50 WALKS IN

Glasgow & South West Scotland

50 WALKS OF 2–10 MILES

First published 2003
Researched, written and updated 2009
by Hugh Taylor and Moira McCrossan

Commissioning Editor: Sandy Draper
Senior Editor: Penny Fowler
Designer: Tracey Butler
Picture Research: Vivien Little
Proofreader: Suzanne Juby
Cartography provided by the Mapping
Services Department of AA Publishing

Produced by AA Publishing
© AA Media Limited 2009

Published by AA Publishing (a trading
name of AA Media Limited, whose
registered office is Fanum House, Basing
View, Basingstoke, Hampshire RG21 4EA;
registered number 06112600)

Enabled by | Ordnance Survey This product includes
mapping data licensed
from the Ordnance Survey® with the
permission of the Controller of Her
Majesty's Stationery Office. © Crown
Copyright 2009. All rights reserved.
Licence number 100021153.

A03628

ISBN: 978-0-7495-6290-8
ISBN: 978-0-7495-6322-6

A CIP catalogue record for this book
is available from the British Library.

Visit AA Publishing at theAA.com/bookshop

Cover reproduction by Keenes
Group, Andover
Printed by Printer Trento Srl, Italy

Acknowledgements
The Automobile Association wishes to
thank the following photographers and
organisations for their assistance in the
preparation of this book.

Abbreviations for the picture credits are as
follows – (AA) AA World Travel Library

3 AA/S Anderson; 9 AA/L Campbell; 13
AA/M Alexander; 18 AA/M Alexander; 40/41
AA/J Beazley; 86/87 A/P and G Bowater;
110/111 Photolibrary Group; 114/115
AA/J Smith; 128/129 AA/D W Robertson;
140/141 AA/D Forss

Illustrations by Andrew Hutchinson

Every effort has been made to trace the
copyright holders, and we apologise in
advance for any accidental errors. We
would be happy to apply any corrections in
the following edition of this publication.

Authors' Acknowledgements
Hugh Taylor and Moira McCrossan would
like to thank Moira Dyer of Glasgow and
Clyde Valley Tourist Board and Mike Blair
of Caledonian MacBrayne for facilities
and information. Archibald W Taylor and
George Hood for background information
on shepherds and the lace industry and
David Hunter FSA Scot for information
on Kirsty McTaggart.

Right: Glen Trool in autumn, Galloway Forest Park (Walk 10)

50 WALKS IN
Glasgow & South West Scotland

50 WALKS OF 2–10 MILES

Contents

WALK		RATING	DISTANCE	PAGE
1	CAERLAVEROCK	+++	5.25 miles (8.4km)	10
2	CARSETHORN	+++	5.5 miles (8.8km)	14
3	NEW ABBEY	+++	3.75 miles (6km)	17
4	NEW ABBEY	+++	7.75 miles (12.5km)	21
5	DUMFRIES	+++	5.5 miles (8.8km)	22
6	GLENKILN	+++	4 miles (6.4km)	24
7	MONIAIVE	+++	5 miles (8km)	27
8	WANLOCKHEAD	+++	3.75 miles (6km)	30
9	LEADHILLS	+++	7.25 miles (11.7km)	33
10	GLENTROOL	+++	5 miles (8km)	34
11	LOCH ENOCH	+++	9 miles (14.5km)	36
12	WIGTOWN	+++	4 miles (6.4km)	39
13	WELLS OF THE REES	+++	6.25 miles (10.1km)	44
14	WELLS OF THE REES	+++	7.5 miles (12km)	47
15	CASTLE KENNEDY	+++	6 miles (9.7km)	48
16	PORT LOGAN	+++	2.5 miles (4km)	50
17	BALLANTRAE	+++	3 miles (4.8km)	53
18	BYNE HILL	+++	3.75 miles (6km)	56
19	KILRANNY	+++	4.25 miles (6.8km)	59
20	BARR	+++	8 miles (12.9km)	60
21	DUNASKIN	+++	4 miles (6.4km)	62
22	MUIRKIRK	+++	3.5 miles (5.7km)	65
23	DARVEL	+++	7 miles (11.3km)	68
24	NEWMILNS	+++	11.5 miles (18.5km)	71
25	LOUDOUN	+++	7.5 miles (12.1km)	72
26	EAST KILBRIDE	+++	5 miles (8km)	74
27	WHITING BAY	+++	2.75 miles (4.4km)	77
28	MACHRIE MOOR	+++	5.5 miles (8.8km)	80
29	BLACKWATERFOOT	+++	5.5 miles (8.8km)	83
30	GLASGOW	+++	2.5 miles (4km)	84

Contents

WALK		RATING	DISTANCE	PAGE
31	GLASGOW	+++	6.5 miles (10.4km)	88
32	CARBETH	+++	3 miles (4.8km)	91
33	CLYDESIDE	+++	4.75 miles (7.7km)	94
34	CLYDESIDE	+++	5.75 miles (9.2km)	97
35	KILSYTH	+++	3.5 miles (5.7km)	98
36	THE WHANGIE	+++	2.5 miles (4km)	100
37	QUEEN ELIZABETH FOREST PARK	+++	4 miles (6.4km)	103
38	ABERFOYLE	+++	3.5 miles (5.7km)	106
39	ABERFOYLE	+++	6 miles (9.7km)	109
40	ABERFOYLE	+++	2 miles (3.2km)	112
41	LOCH LOMOND	+++	2 miles (3.2km)	116
42	BALQUHIDDER	+++	2.5 miles (4km)	119
43	LOCH KATRINE	+++	6.75 miles (10.9km)	122
44	LOCH KATRINE	+++	6 miles (9.7km)	125
45	REST AND BE THANKFUL	+++	4.5 miles (7.2km)	126
46	BENMORE	+++	4 miles (6.4km)	130
47	DUNARDRY FOREST	+++	8.25 miles (13.3km)	133
48	KILMARTIN GLEN	+++	3.5 miles (5.7km)	136
49	KILMARTIN GLEN	+++	6.25 miles (10.1km)	139
50	CARRADALE FOREST	+++	6 miles (9.7km)	142

Rating

Each walk is rated for its relative difficulty compared to the other walks in this book. Walks marked +++ are likely to be shorter and easier with little total ascent. The hardest walks are marked +++

Walking in Safety

For advice and safety tips see page 144.

Locator Map

Legend

	Walk Route		Built-up Area
1	Route Waypoint		Woodland Area
– – –	Adjoining Path	👬	Toilet
⚡	Viewpoint	P	Car Park
•	Place of Interest	🪑	Picnic Area
⌂	Steep Section	)(	Bridge

Introducing Glasgow & South West Scotland

The quiet south-west is a good place to start exploring Scotland, from the gently rolling pastures of Dumfriesshire to 'Grey Galloway' with its windswept moors, secluded byways and the rugged Galloway Hills. There are walks in these hills that are every bit as remote and taxing as anything you'll encounter in the Highlands but without the height. The Southern Uplands Way, from Port Patrick in the far west, cuts across the grain of the country and is probably the most difficult long distance footpath in Scotland. Tramp a section of this across open moor and you'll quickly realise why the hill folk of the south-west were such a hardy breed.

Cross into Ayrshire and rugged Galloway fades into a pastoral landscape. The coastline of the west is bordered by fertile fields, created from raised beaches, famous for their early potatoes. Once the entire county was covered in moor and bog. Agricultural improvements and extensive drainage in the 17th and 18th centuries created today's farmland. Inland, and in remote parts of the county, areas of bog and moor still exist. It was from bleak land like this that subsistence farmers and miners scratched a living. Yet many who became household names came from this background. Farmer's son, Alexander Fleming went on to discover penicillin while miner, Bill Shankly, who learned his sporting skills in the village of Glenbuck, became a footballing legend.

Ayrshire gives way to Glasgow and the central belt. The City of Glasgow has risen from the ashes of soot-blackened slums to become the greatest shopping experience north of London. It also revels in the distinction of having been European City of Culture and Architecture, with a rich heritage of Victorian buildings and imaginative modern designs.

Heading north, Loch Lomond was close enough to Glasgow for many of the slum dwellers of the depression years to escape the grind of dirt and poverty and breathe in the freedom of the hills. From here, and east through the beautiful countryside of the Trossachs, is Scotland's first National Park.

A few hundred years ago cattle rustlers roamed here and the outlawed Rob Roy MacGregor evaded capture for years amongst the dense heather on these hillsides. The hardy Glasgow outdoor types of the 1930s slept amongst this heather while they enjoyed the scenery. They also tramped to the west of Loch Lomond to the area around Tarbert, which

PUBLIC TRANSPORT

Glasgow is well served by an extensive rail network and a small underground known as the Clockwork Orange. The railways are reasonably extensive in the Greater Glasgow area but further afield, particularly in the south-west, rail travel varies from sparse to non-existent (Strathclyde Partnership for Transport 0141 332 6811 or www.spt.co.uk). Details of the public bus network are available from www.stagecoachbus.com and 0871 200 2233. CalMac ferries serve the island of Arran and the Kintyre and Cowal peninsulas (information from 08000 66 5000 or www.calmac.co.uk).

they named the Arrochar Alps. Here they learned the skills that would take some of them to the summits of the world's highest mountains.

The road to Argyll was constructed by Major Caufield after the Jacobite rising of 1745 and stretches of the original road still remain. Argyll is one of the oldest areas of settlement in Scotland. It was here that the Scotti first settled from Ireland and established the kingdom that is now known as Scotland. Further up that glen, earlier inhabitants left evidence of their story in the valley in stone monuments, astronomical sites and cemeteries.

This book is a walk through Scotland's story, from the ancient Celts, to the artistic, literary and scientific greats of the 19th and 20th centuries. It tells of the people, who lived, worked, played and died on this soil and of the land itself, challenging and majestic, beautiful and yet also treacherous.

Using this book

Information Panels

An information panel for each walk shows its relative difficulty (see page 5), the distance and total amount of ascent. An indication of the gradients you will encounter is shown by the rating ✦✦✦ (no steep slopes) to ✦✦✦ (several very steep slopes).

Maps

There are 30 maps, covering 40 of the walks. Some walks have a suggested option in the same area. The information panel for these walks will tell you how much extra walking is involved. On short-cut suggestions the panel will tell you the total distance if you set out from the start of the main walk. Where an option returns to the same point on the main walk, just the distance of the loop is given. Where an option leaves the main walk at one point and returns to it at another, then the distance shown is for the whole walk. The minimum time suggested is for reasonably fit walkers and doesn't allow for stops. Each walk has a suggested map.

Start Points

The start of each walk is given as a six-figure grid reference prefixed by two letters indicating which 100km square of the National Grid it refers to. You'll find more information on grid references on most Ordnance Survey maps.

Dogs

We have tried to give dog owners useful advice about how dog friendly each walk is. Please respect other countryside users. Keep your dog under control, especially around livestock, and obey local bylaws and other dog control notices.

Car Parking

Many of the car parks suggested are public, but occasionally you may find you have to park on the roadside or in a lay-by. Please be considerate when you leave your car, ensuring that access roads or gates are not blocked and that other vehicles can pass safely.

Right: Red squirrel (Sciurus vulgaris) in a wood on the Scottish Borders

Caerlaverock Castle and the Solway Merses

*A ramble taking in an ancient fortress
and a National Nature Reserve.*

WALK 1

DISTANCE 5.25 miles (8.4km)   **MINIMUM TIME** 2hrs 30min

ASCENT/GRADIENT 82ft (25m) ▲▲▲   **LEVEL OF DIFFICULTY** ✦✦✦

PATHS Country lanes, farm tracks and salt marsh, 1 stile

LANDSCAPE Pastures, salt marsh, riverside and hills

SUGGESTED MAP OS Explorer 314 Solway Firth

START/FINISH Grid reference: NY 051656

DOG FRIENDLINESS Keep on lead while on reserve

PARKING Car park at Wildfowl and Wetlands Trust Reserve

PUBLIC TOILETS At Wildfowl and Wetlands Trust Reserve

Against the impressive backdrop of Criffel, guarded by the wide waters of the Solway Firth, the salt marshes and the impressive medieval castle of Caerlaverock, this out-of-the-way corner of Scotland is a haven for wildlife and a treasure trove of history.

A Castle Under Siege

Caerlaverock, the Castle of the Lark, was once the main gatekeeper to south-west Scotland. Protected by mudflats and the shifting channels of the sea, it was vulnerable only from the landward side. During the Scottish Wars of Independence (1286–1370) it was attacked frequently. From the siege of Caerlaverock by Edward I in 1300 through to the 17th century it was continually beseiged, levelled and rebuilt. Its garrison last surrendered in 1640. Partially demolished, it crumbled to an ivy-covered ruin until restoration in the mid-20th century. Within the ruined walls of this triangular fortress, conservators continue their work on one of the finest Renaissance residences in Scotland.

Preserving the Balance

Conservation work of a different kind takes place on the merse (salt marsh) that bounds the Solway coast. Here Scottish Natural Heritage (SNH), the Wildfowl and Wetlands Trust (WWT) and the Caerlaverock Estate work at preserving the delicate balance that allows farming and wild fowling to exist alongside a National Nature Reserve.

The desolate open spaces, unchanged for centuries, echo to the cry of the wild geese in winter, the oystercatcher and heron in summer and the mating chorus of the natterjack toad in spring. But it wasn't always so. Wildfowling had seriously reduced the goose population to a few hundred in 1957, when the local landowner, the Duke of Norfolk, agreed to divide the merse into an area for controlled shooting and a wildlife sanctuary, now the National Nature Reserve. This is also one of the last places in Britain where scientists can study the important natural processes of growth and erosion of salt marshes.

CAERLAVEROCK

Sir Peter Scott

In 1970 the Duke offered the naturalist, Sir Peter Scott, the lease of Eastpark Farm for the WWT. Here, every October, the Spitsbergen population of barnacle geese fly in from Norway to their winter quarters along the merse. The birds can be seen from specially constructed hides along roads shielded with high hedges to minimise disturbance to wildlife.

Whooper swans overwinter here too, along with the pink-footed goose, pintail, scaup, oystercatcher, knot, bar-tailed godwit, curlew and redshank. Staff at Eastpark organise a variety of events to help visitors appreciate the reserve, including birding, natterjack toad and bat spotting, and pond dipping. As part of the conservation process, wildfowling is permitted in winter. Barnacle geese are protected but other species are fair game. The wildfowlers are experts at recognition and SNH wardens ensure fair play.

WALK 1 DIRECTIONS

❶ Exit the car park and turn right on to a farm road. Follow this past the farms of Newfield and Midtown then turn left and go past a bungalow and some houses. Just before you reach the farm of Hollands there is a waymarker pointing to a car park, on the right, and straight ahead for walks. Go straight ahead and continue to the farm steading, then turn left.

2 Go through a gate and on to a farm track. This stretches away into the distance and has high hedges on both sides. Continue along this track between the hedges and on, over an overgrown section, until you reach the end. Then turn right at the signpost indicating Caerlaverock.

3 A sign here informs visitors that regulated wildfowling (shooting) takes place between 1 September to 20 February. Follow the rough track through the grass along the edge of the merse in the direction of the arrow on the footpath waymarker post. The path can be very boggy at all times and the grass will be high in the summer.

> ### WHILE YOU'RE THERE
> The Dumfries Museum and Camera Obscura is housed in a former windmill and has a comprehensive collection covering the history of the region, its people and wildlife. Here you'll see fossils, stone carvings by early Christians, a range of Victoriana, some death masks, a plaster cast of the skull of Robert Burns and the first writings of J M Barrie who lived in Dumfries for a time.

4 The path through the nature reserve varies from faint to non-existent; Wellington boots are recommended. It splits at several points and then meanders back and forth, but all the lines of the path rejoin and you'll end up at the same place whichever one you decide to take.

5 Eventually some cottages can be seen in the field to the right. Bear right, through a gate and into the field. Walk to the left around the field perimeter, past some cottages, then turn left through a gate to emerge on to a farm track,

> ### WHERE TO EAT AND DRINK
> There's an excellent family-friendly café and tea room in Eastpark (WWT Visitor Centre). It is bright and spacious and serves a good range of hot food, snacks and cakes. It also houses the WWT gift and bookshop.

passing a sign for Caerlaverock Castle and into the castle grounds.

6 Follow the road past the old castle, which has been excavated and has information boards to explain the ruins, and go through a wood with nature trail information boards to Caerlaverock Castle. There is a children's playground, a siege machine and picnic tables around the ramparts of the castle.

> ### WHAT TO LOOK OUT FOR
> While on the salt marsh and mudflats section of this walk the large hill immediately in front of you is Criffel (see Walk 3). Look out along here for grebes and wintering goldeneye and in the spring for the black-tailed godwit on passage. In spring and summer this area is particularly rich in wild flowers. You'll need to carry a field guide with you to get the most from the walk.

7 At the far end go through an arch and continue to the T-junction with a country lane. Turn right and continue for about a mile (1.6km), then turn right on to another lane signposted 'Wildfowl and Wetlands Reserve'. Continue on this road past the farms of Northpark, Newmains and Nethertown and then back to the car park at Eastpark.

Opposite: The ruins of Caerlaverock Castle dating largely from the 15th century (Walk 1)

The Solway Shore from Carsethorn to Arbigland

Visit the birthplace of John Paul Jones,
the 'father of the American Navy'.

DISTANCE 5.5 miles (8.8km)	**MINIMUM TIME** 2hrs 30min
ASCENT/GRADIENT 82ft (25m) ▲▲▲	**LEVEL OF DIFFICULTY** ✦✦✦
PATHS Rocky seashore, woodland tracks and country road	
LANDSCAPE Seashore, woodland and pasture	
SUGGESTED MAP OS Explorer 313 Dumfries & Dalbeattie, New Abbey	
START/FINISH Grid reference: NX 993598	
DOG FRIENDLINESS Good walk for dogs	
PARKING Car park by beach at Carsethorn	
PUBLIC TOILETS At John Paul Jones Museum	

The man hailed in the USA as the 'father of the American Navy' was born John Paul in a poor gardener's cottage at Arbigland, on the Solway coast in 1745.

Young Seaman

At the age of 13 John signed up as an apprentice seaman journeying to Virginia on the *Friendship of Whitehaven*. He later signed on as third mate on a slave ship, the *King George of Whitehaven*. He lasted two years and advanced to first mate before he quit in disgust with the slave trade. On his passage home he acquired his first command when the captain and mate of his vessel died of fever. As the only qualified man left, John took control and brought the ship safely home. The owners rewarded him with permanent command. He had a reputation for a fiery temper and was once charged with murder but found not guilty. In 1773 he fled the West Indies, after killing the ringleader of a mutiny, and went to Virginia. It was around this time that he changed his name to John Paul Jones.

American Naval Officer

In the lead up to the American Revolution (War of American Independence) when Congress was forming a 'Continental Navy', Jones offered his services and was commissioned as a first lieutenant on the *Alfred* in 1775. Later, as captain of the *Providence*, he advised Congress on naval regulations. In 1778, after a daring hit-and-run raid on Whitehaven, he sailed across the Solway to Kirkcudbright Bay to kidnap the Earl of Selkirk and ransom him for American captives. However the earl was not at home and the raiding party had to be content with looting the family silver.

Famous Battle

In September 1779, as commodore of a small squadron of French ships, John Paul Jones engaged his ship the *Bonhomme Richard* with the superior HMS *Serapis* and HMS *Countess of Scarborough* off Flamborough Head. After a dreadful four-hour fight, in which Jones was injured and his ship sunk, he

CARSETHORN

eventually won the battle, transferred his crew to the *Serapis* and sailed for Holland with his prisoners and booty.

John Paul Jones died in France in 1792 and his body lay in an unmarked grave for over a century. His remains were eventually taken back to the USA amid great ceremony and he was finally laid to rest in the chapel crypt of the Annapolis Naval Academy in 1913.

WALK 2 DIRECTIONS

1 From the car park at Carsethorn head down on to the beach and turn right. Continue walking along the shore for approximately 2 miles (3.2km). The beach at this point is sandy and may be strewn with driftwood, but if the tide has come in you will be walking over more rocky ground.

2 After you reach The House on the Shore, which is beside the beach on your right, continue around the small headland and along the beach to the next one, then look for a faint path heading uphill to join a well-defined track that heads alongside a stone wall.

3 Continue along this track and then descend steeply to arrive at the beach beside an impressive natural rock arch called the Thirl Stane. You can go through the arch to the sea if the tide is in, although if the tide is out on this part of the coast, the sea will be far off in the distance.

4 Continue from here along the rocks on the pebble shore and up a grassy bank until you reach a car park. Exit the car park on to a lane. Continue on the lane past Powillimount. Turn right when you get to a lodge house on the right-hand side and walk along the estate road to reach the cottage birthplace of John Paul Jones.

5 There is a fascinating small museum here. Continue along the road past the gates to Arbigland, on to the road signed 'No vehicular traffic'. Follow the road as it turns right and along the side of some of the Arbigland Estate buildings.

6 When the road turns left at a cottage, go right on to a dirt track. Follow the dirt track until it emerges on to a surfaced road next to Tallowquhairn to your right. Take the road away from the farm, turning sharply left around some houses, then right and continue to a T-junction.

7 Turn right and follow this road round to the left. Follow the long straight road as far as the right turn to South Carse. Go along the farm road and straight through the farm steading as far as you can go, then turn left.

8 To return to the shore again, walk along a footpath passing a brightly coloured caravan and the rear of some cottages. Look out for a narrow track heading downhill to the right, giving access to the beach. Turn left along the beach to the car park.

Criffel and New Abbey

*A 13th-century love story of the Lady Devorgilla,
set forever in stone.*

DISTANCE *3.75 miles (6km)*   MINIMUM TIME *3hrs*

ASCENT/GRADIENT *1,686ft (514m)* ▲▲▲   LEVEL OF DIFFICULTY +++

PATHS *Forest road, rough hill and wood tracks, 1 stile*

LANDSCAPE *Hills, tidal estuary, woods and pasture*

SUGGESTED MAP *OS Explorer 313 Dumfries & Dalbeattie*

START/FINISH *Grid reference: NX 971634*

DOG FRIENDLINESS *Keep on lead near livestock*

PARKING *Car park at Ardwall farm*

PUBLIC TOILETS *None en route*

The majestic ruins of Sweetheart Abbey dominate the village of New Abbey. Set against the backdrop of Criffel, Dumfries's highest hill, they stand as testimony to one woman's love, devotion and determination.

A Lasting Memorial

Sweetheart Abbey was founded in 1273 by Devorgilla, Lady of Galloway, as a memorial to her late husband, John Balliol, and as a last resting place for them both. When Balliol died at Barnard Castle in 1269, Devorgilla had his heart removed from his corpse, embalmed and placed in a silver-mounted ivory casket which she carried everywhere with her.

Devorgilla lived long enough to see the abbey rise beside the River Nith. She died in 1289 at Barnard Castle, Durham, and her body was carried to Dumfries, her last journey following that of her husband through the north of England into Scotland. She was interred at Sweetheart Abbey, next to her husband near the high altar, and the cask containing his heart was placed on her breast. Her devotion and attachment to her husband led the monks to give the abbey the name *dulce cor* or sweet heart. Within the abbey there can still be seen a, now headless, effigy of her holding the casket.

Originally the abbey was called New Abbey, to distinguish it from the nearby mother house of Dundrennan, and so the village that subsequently grew up around it took its name. At the Reformation, supported by the local population and the powerful Maxwell family, the abbot, Gilbert Brown, refused to give up the abbey. Eventually, in 1610, after two evictions and arrests, he was finally sent into exile.

The villagers had considerable affection for the abbey and, in 1779, started a fund to ensure its preservation. Now under the care of Historic Scotland, it remains one of the most impressive abbey ruins in Scotland. Although the roof has gone, the cruciform church and massive central tower, built from red Dumfriesshire sandstone, still stand.

The monks of Dundrennan, Glenluce and New Abbey were members of the Order of the Cistercians founded in 1098 at Cîteaux in Burgundy. Directed by the rule of St Benedict they observed a life of poverty, chastity

NEW ABBEY

and obedience. In 1136, some white monks of this order travelled north from Rievaulx, in Yorkshire, to found the abbey at Melrose and six years later came to Dundrennan. Although they lived an austere life, the Cistercians played an important part in the trading network. They were the largest producers of wool in the country, at their peak accounting for around 5 per cent of Scotland's total wool production. They provided employment and helped establish towns and burghs throughout the country.

WALK 3 DIRECTIONS

❶ Exit the car park via a kissing gate, cross a farm road and then go through another kissing gate and continue along a track. Turn right after 70yds (64m) then head towards the hill on a track between dry-stone walls. When the road starts to curve left, in front of the wood, take the rough track off to the right.

Opposite: The setting sun causes the rich, red sandstone of Sweetheart Abbey to glow (Walks 3 and 4)

2 Follow a track uphill through the trees following by the Craigrockall Burn. It narrows in places and the ground is very uneven with several large boulders to climb over or around.

3 When you reach a T-junction with a forest road, keep straight ahead to pick up the trail on the other side and continue uphill. Cross another forest road and eventually reach a fence. Cross the fence and veer to the left, heading towards the summit of Criffel.

WHILE YOU'RE THERE

There's an opportunity to see how oatmeal and flour were produced at New Abbey Corn Mill. This classic example of a Galloway country mill is the last survivor of a once common-place industry. The fully restored, working, 18th-century mill is powered by a waterwheel and offers regular demonstrations of the miller's trade.

4 From the trig point you'll have a superb view. Across the Solway to the south is England and the hills of the Lake District. A little to the right of that is the Isle of Man, while the coast of Ireland is visible to the west. The ancient Scotti tribe came from Ireland and founded Scotland. On a good day the summit of Criffel is the best restaurant in town, provided you have remembered to pack the food. When you've eaten your picnic and enjoyed the view (see What To Look Out For) head roughly north-west from the cairn, following a faint path that leads towards the broad ridge that runs from Criffel to the neighbouring hill of Knockendoch. Head downhill, then continue, ascending again, to the summit of Knockendoch.

WHERE TO EAT AND DRINK

Conveniently situated right at the entrance to Sweetheart Abbey is the Abbey Cottage tea room where visitors can enjoy anything from a cup of tea and a scone to snacks and light meals. Elsewhere in New Abbey its worth taking the time to check out the 19th-century, Tudor-style Criffel Inn with its superb selection of cask beers and over 120 malt whiskies. The atmospheric bar is also the best place to sample their excellent meals, freshly prepared using local produce.

5 From the summit cairn head east and go downhill. In the summer, when the heather is particularly thick, the going can be fairly tough and you'll have to proceed slowly and with caution. Make for the fence that runs across the hill in front of you. Turn right here and follow it back to the point you crossed on the way up, then and retrace your steps to the bottom of the hill.

WHAT TO LOOK OUT FOR

From the summit of Criffel look east towards Caerlaverock Castle on the opposite bank of the River Nith. Beyond that you will be able to see a nature reserve among the Solway Merses and beyond that a patchwork of lush, rolling pastures, marked out by ancient dry-stone walls.

Knochendoch to New Abbey

It's downhill most of the way to Devorgilla's Sweetheart Abbey.
See map and information panel for Walk 3

DISTANCE *7.75 miles (12.5km)* MINIMUM TIME *6hrs*
ASCENT/GRADIENT *1,768ft (539m)* ▲▲▲ LEVEL OF DIFFICULTY +++

WALK 4 DIRECTIONS
(Walk 3 option)

From the summit of Knochendoch (Point **A**) head roughly north and pick up a rough path heading downhill with a wall on the left. Continue to descend following the wall to a corner with a fence and cross a stile on the left. Continue downhill from here with the wall on your right. Look up, ahead and to the left for a tower-like building on top of Waterloo Hill. This monument commemorates the Battle of Waterloo.

Access to the monument from New Abbey is by an easy walk on the minor road to Mid Glen and then by footpath up the hill. Some 49ft (15m) high, the monument has a winding stone staircase inside, leading to the top where you can enjoy views of the village, Dumfries, Caerlaverock and Shambellie House museum. According to the inscription it was built in 1816 to 'record the valour of those British, Belgian and Prussian soldiers who under Wellington and Blutcher on the 18th of June 1815 gained the victory at Waterloo by which French tyranny was overthrown and peace restored to the world'.

This is fairly typical of the many Waterloo monuments built at the time and conveys some impression of the impact the Napoleonic Wars had on the area.

Continue carefully on the descending path as the ground is very boggy until you enter a larch forest where the surface becomes firmer. Shortly clear the forest and the path ends at a junction with a forest road. Turn right, follow the road, crossing a stile, a gate and a bridge. Do not go through the gate at the end of the bridge but turn right and continue on the road.

Look out on the grass verges and ditches by the roadside for a variety of wild flowers including the heath spotted orchid, a profusion of lesser celandine, foxgloves, red campion and a variety of ferns.

From here go through another four gates and, shortly after the last one, go right when the path forks to join the drive to Barbeth farm. Go through a set of gates at the end of the road to arrive in New Abbey (Point **B**). Follow this road through the village to the A710 then turn right. Walk for about 2 miles (3.2km) to the turn off to Ardwall farm on the right. Turn up here and return to the car park at the start.

A Dumfries Town Trail

In the footsteps of Burns and Barrie around the birthplace of Peter Pan.

DISTANCE *5.5 miles (8.8km)*   MINIMUM TIME *2hrs*

ASCENT/GRADIENT *Negligible* ▲▲▲   LEVEL OF DIFFICULTY ✦✦✦

PATHS *Pavements*

LANDSCAPE *Town streets and river bank*

SUGGESTED MAP *OS Explorer 313 Dumfries & Dalbeattie, New Abbey*

START/FINISH *Grid reference: NX 976765*

DOG FRIENDLINESS *Keep on lead*

PARKING *Dumfries Station*

PUBLIC TOILETS *Dumfries Station*

WALK 5 DIRECTIONS

With the railway station behind you turn left. Leave the car park, turn left at the Waverley Hotel and go over the railway bridge. Go over a roundabout and then turn left when you reach Victoria Terrace, a handsome row of substantial houses with their gardens across the road. Barrie lived at No 6, as an engraving on the wall testifies: 'Sir James Mathew Barrie BART OM 1860–1937, Scottish novelist and dramatist. J M Barrie lived in this house, the home of his brother, while a scholar at Dumfries Academy from 1873 to 1878. He regarded his stay in Dumfries as among his happiest days. In

WHERE TO EAT AND DRINK

Hulabaloo, which is part of the Robert Burns Centre, is one of the best places to eat in Dumfries. The emphasis is on fresh Scottish ingredients with a world food slant. The home-made soup is delicious as are the filled rolls, with a choice of breads, salads and constantly changing main courses.

1924 he was made a freeman of Dumfries the town where Peter Pan was born.'

Retrace your steps to the road and turn right. Go back across the roundabout and continue past the Waverley Hotel, the traffic lights and the County Buildings until you come to Shakespeare Street on your left. Cross the road and turn into it. Pass the Theatre Royal, where Burns was a patron, and turn left into Burns Street.

The street winds uphill, passing Burns House on the left, then reaches a junction next to a statue of Burns' wife, Jean Armour. Cross the road to St Michael's Church and visit the Burns Mausoleum in the churchyard. Retrace your footsteps to the top of Burns Street and continue down Nith Place. Turn right in front of the Loreburn Centre then turn left into the pedestrian area of the High Street.

Look out for the sign and entrance close of the Globe Inn, to the right, opposite Marks and Spencer, and go in to visit Burns' favourite

DUMFRIES

haunt. Here he would regularly hold court of an evening and if he had a few too many would often stay overnight in the room upstairs. You can try his personal chair for size, but be warned that anyone who sits here who can't recite some of the bard's work must stand the rest of the company a drink. In the upstairs bedroom Burns scratched a few verses of poetry on the window pane and they can still be seen.

Come back through the close and turn right. Head past the fountain in the direction of the Mid Steeple and turn left down Bank Street. Near the bottom of the street look up on the right for a couple of plaques, which identify the building Burns and his family moved to in 1791 when they vacated Ellisland Farm. Here, over 18 months, he wrote more than 60 songs including the poignant love song 'Ae Fond Kiss'.

Continue to the Whitesands and cross the road to the banks of the Nith. Turn left and walk beside the river to the suspension bridge. Turn right and cross the bridge, head up Suspension Brae and turn right on to Troqueer Road. Head uphill to the Dumfries Museum and Camera Obscura, housed in an old windmill. Here, if you ask, you can see the earliest known example of Barrie's writing, *Rekollections of a Skoolmaster*, which was published in a school magazine produced by one of Barrie's childhood friends.

Continue past the museum and, at the end of a block of sandstone buildings on your right, turn right and go down some steps to reach the Robert Burns Centre. Exit the Burns Centre, and turn right along the riverside to the ancient Devorgilla's Bridge, which you cross to reach the Whitesands again. Cross the road and make your way up Friars Vennel. Turn left at the top, pass Burns Statue and cross the road to Greyfriars' Church. Go to the left of the church along Castle Street and turn right at the crossroads.

Continue to the last house on the left, opposite the entrance to Dumfries Academy. This is Moat Brae, former home of Barrie's friend Wellwood (Wed) Anderson. It was here that the tale of *Peter Pan* was born as Barrie and friends played pirates in the garden.

From here go along Irvine Street, turn left at the junction and along the front of Dumfries Academy where Barrie went to school. At the second set of traffic-lights turn right into Lovers Walk to return to the railway station.

WALK 6

The Glenkiln Outdoor Sculptures

Discover the works of Henry Moore, Epstein and Rodin in a unique countryside setting.

DISTANCE 4 miles (6.4km)	**MINIMUM TIME** 2hrs 30min
ASCENT/GRADIENT 312ft (95m) ▲▲▲	**LEVEL OF DIFFICULTY** +++

PATHS Country roads, farm tracks, open hillside

LANDSCAPE Sculptures, hills, woodland and reservoir

SUGGESTED MAP OS Explorer 321 Nithsdale & Dumfries

START/FINISH Grid reference: NX 839784

DOG FRIENDLINESS Keep on lead on farmland, particularly at lambing time

PARKING Car park in front of statue of John the Baptist

PUBLIC TOILETS None en route or near by

During the mid-1950s Tony Keswick, a Dumfriesshire landowner with a penchant for sculpture, acquired a copy of August Rodin's *John the Baptist* from the Musée Rodin in Paris. Keswick did not hide it away in a darkened vault or even in a gallery. It stands today, as it always has, in open countryside, atop a hillock, its outstretched arm beckoning across the water of Glenkiln Reservoir.

An Amazing Collection

Keswick was given the hill farm of Glenkiln by his father in 1924 as a 21st birthday present but he rarely visited it until the 1950s. That first Rodin was the start of an amazing collection of art. On a visit to the studio of Henry Moore, he immediately recognised that Moore's *Standing Figure* would be ideal placed on a large flat boulder that stood by the roadside near the farm. This was followed by Moore's *King and Queen*. Of the six casts made, the Glenkiln piece is the only one in a private collection. Keswick tried a number of sites around his land before placing it on a hillside overlooking the reservoir. The sculptures look out serenely over their domain, separate from, yet part of the landscape that surrounds them.

Hard Times

Epstein's *Visitation* is in the collection of the Tate Gallery in London. Keswick obtained Epstein's own copy purely by chance. He was with the artist when a group of workmen arrived to cart the work off to melt it down. Epstein, although famous, was so hard up that he was selling some of his work for scrap to pay the foundry bill for a bust of Winston Churchill he was working on. Keswick was appalled and promptly bought the statue. It depicts the Virgin Mary with folded hands, head slightly bowed and an expression of utmost serenity on her face. She's located a bit off the beaten track and surrounded by Scots pine within the tumbledown walls of a long abandoned sheep fold. To stumble, seemingly almost by accident, on this figure, particularly on a slightly dark and misty winter's day, when the sheep have gathered around her, is one of the magical moments of Glenkiln.

GLENKILN

Glenkiln has been a popular attraction since Tony Keswick placed his first sculpture out of doors. He positively encouraged people to come and see the collection and today it remains as a tribute not just to the work of the artists but to the memory of a remarkable man who saw sculpture as a complement to nature.

WALK 6 DIRECTIONS

❶ From the car park in front of the statue *John the Baptist*, return to the main road and turn right. Cross a cattle grid then turn right and go past the statue to the Marglolly Burn. Turn left and walk along the bank towards Cornlee Bridge. Just before the bridge turn left and head back to the road. You'll come across Henry Moore's

Standing Figure before you at the junction with a farm road.

❷ Turn left and head back along the main road. Just before the entrance to Margreig farm on the right is a muddy track running across the field to a gate in the dry-stone wall. Head up and through the gate then keep straight ahead, uphill and towards a telephone pole. At the pole veer

25

left and follow the track uphill. The Glenkiln Cross should now be visible in front of you.

❸ There are several footpaths and tracks available here. Take the one that is closest to a large tree in front of you. Cross over a burn at the tree and then take the path that skirts to the left of it. Veer right and then head for the high ground. Once the cross comes into view again continue ahead directly towards it.

❹ From the cross turn to face Glenkiln Reservoir and then head downhill towards a telephone pole. Go through a gate in the fence at the bottom of the hill and then turn right on to the road. After a short distance along here a farm track leads uphill to the right. Go through a gate and on to it. To your right on the hillside is Henry Moore's *King and Queen*.

❺ Continue on this track. Go through a gate, pass a small wooded area on your right and then bare hillside until you spot a small stand of Scots pine on the

left. Leave the road at this point and continue to the trees and Epstein's *Visitation*. Return to the road and then continue to the end where you go through a gate, cross over a bridge then turn left on to the road.

❻ Go downhill on this road for 0.5 mile (800m), crossing a cattle grid. Just before the end of the conifer plantation on the left, look out for Moore's *Two Piece Reclining Figure No 1* on your right. Follow the road all the way downhill from here, turn left at the junction and continue on this road until you reach the car park.

The Last Turning in Moniaive

The village that inspired the 19th-century school of artists known as the Glasgow Boys.

DISTANCE 5 miles (8km)	MINIMUM TIME 3hrs
ASCENT/GRADIENT 295ft (90m) ▲▲▲	LEVEL OF DIFFICULTY ✦✦✦

PATHS Dirt roads, hill tracks, forest road and country lane

LANDSCAPE Hills and woodland

SUGGESTED MAP OS Explorers 321 Nithsdale & Dumfries, Thornhill; 328 Sanquhar & New Cumnock, Muirkirk

START/FINISH Grid reference: NX 780910 (on Explorer 328)

DOG FRIENDLINESS Keep on lead near livestock

PARKING Moniaive village car park

PUBLIC TOILETS Ayr Street, passed on walk

Moniaive is one of Scotland's most picturesque villages and described by *The Times* as 'one of the coolest villages in Britain'. Situated at a crossroads where the waters of three glens meet, it has a natural attraction for artists. James Paterson came here in the summer of 1879, the first of several summer painting visits. When he married in 1884, he decided to settle in Moniaive and moved into Kilneis on the outskirts of the village. Originally a small stone cottage, Paterson's father commissioned the architect John James Burnet to enlarge it as a wedding present to his son and his bride.

A Rebellious Bunch

Paterson was born in Glasgow in 1854 to a prosperous middle class family of cotton and muslin manufacturers. He persuaded his father to make him a small allowance to enable him to study art in Paris. Courting controversy, he became part of the group of painters known as the Glasgow Boys, which included W Y Macgregor, E A Walton and James Guthrie, who would meet at life classes in Macgregor's Glasgow studio. They were a rebellious bunch and detested the moribund traditions of the Royal Scottish Academy (RSA). Influenced by the realism of contemporary French painters, they successfully exhibited in London and throughout Europe while being ignored by the Scottish establishment. In later life their painting became more conservative and Paterson was finally elected to the RSA and became its librarian and secretary.

Landscape Painter

Much of Paterson's finest work was completed in Moniaive. A dedicated landscape painter, he had a wooden studio built on the banks of Craigdarroch Water. Today his watercolours and oils can be found in galleries throughout the world but his most famous work hangs in Glasgow's Kelvingrove Museum and Art Gallery. *The Last Turning* shows a woman in black walking along a country lane. To her left is the water of a mill pond and across it the spire of the clock tower on the schoolmaster's house. The pond is long gone from Moniaive, replaced by a century's growth of trees, but everything else remains the same and in winter it is still possible to glimpse the tower through the trees.

From 1897 Paterson had a studio in Edinburgh and lived for only part of the year in Moniaive. By 1906 he had moved his family permanently to the capital and finally sold Kilneis in 1917. He died in Edinburgh in 1932 but his son, Hamish Constable Paterson, himself an artist, returned to live in Moniaive in 1953. Another Paterson artist, Ann Paterson Wallace opened the James Paterson Museum in the village in the 1990s. Although this subsequently closed, her collection of Paterson memorabilia and Paterson's own photographs are still available for study at Glasgow University's Dumfries Campus.

WALK 7 DIRECTIONS

❶ Exit the car park and turn right. At a nearby T-junction turn right and go over the pedestrian bridge, beside a garage, to enter Moniaive High Street at the George Hotel. Walk along the High Street, past the Market Cross, turn left and cross the road. Turn right when you reach the other side and head up Ayr Street, passing the public toilets.

MONIAIVE

② The building on the right with the clock tower is the former schoolmaster's house. Continue up Ayr Street passing a park on the right and some wooden garages on the left. Take the next right on to a narrow lane. Continue to the end and, at a T-junction, turn right.

WHILE YOU'RE THERE

Visit Kircudbright, an ancient town on the Solway coast west of Dumfries. The light in this part of the world is unique and has always held a fascination for artists. E A Hornel, another of the Glasgow Boys, painted here and eventually set up home in the large Georgian Broughton House, now in the care of the National Trust for Scotland.

---

③ Pass a modern bungalow on the left, then a field, then turn left on to a dirt road at the end of the field. Cross a bridge and continue up the road to Bardennoch. When the road curves right to enter the grounds of the house, go straight on passing a waymarker post and follow the road which goes up the side of the wood and uphill.

④ At the end of the woodland section go through a gate and continue uphill, go through two more gates, and then at the top, near the ruin of Upper Bardennoch, go through another gate. From here continue to climb towards a stand of Scots pine. Head uphill through the trees, following markers, and continue toward another marker on the horizon at Bardennoch Hill.

⑤ From the summit, follow markers. Ahead is woodland and a gate in the wall. Head straight for this or follow the winding track. Go through the gate and keep straight ahead towards a lochan and the start of a forest road.

⑥ Turn right and follow this road downhill through several gates until it reaches a footpath fingerpost at a T-junction with a country lane. Go through a gate, turn right. At the next T-junction a left turn leads to the hamlet of Tynron which is worth visiting. Otherwise turn right again.

WHAT TO LOOK OUT FOR

The lane that runs between Ayr Street and North Street is where James Patterson painted his best-known work *The Last Turning*. When you reach the small house on the left by a bend turn around. To the right, 100 years ago, there was a mill pond instead of trees when the unknown 'woman in black', seen in the painting, was walking along the lane.

---

⑦ Follow this road past Dalmakerran farm then uphill and through a hazel wood. Pass two stone cottages on the right then, further along, another house. The road goes downhill again on to Dunreggan Brae. At the bottom of the hill re-enter Moniaive and turn right into the car park.

WHERE TO EAT AND DRINK

The Green Tea House in Chapel Street welcomes children and serves a wonderful selection of hot meals and snacks, all made from organic ingredients by Catherine Braid – the Organic Country Cook. Try the delicious soups with freshly baked bread, bacon baps with brie, pasta dishes or some of the amazing sweet and sticky things washed down with tea or coffee from a cup the size of a soup bowl.

Wanlockhead: Scotland's Highest Village

Discover the secrets of lead and gold mining in 'God's Treasure House'.

WALK

8

DISTANCE 3.75 miles (6km)   **MINIMUM TIME** 3hrs

ASCENT/GRADIENT 525ft (160m) ▲▲▲   **LEVEL OF DIFFICULTY** ✦✦✦

PATHS Footpaths, hill tracks, hillside and old railway lines, 1 stile

LANDSCAPE Hills, mining relics and village

SUGGESTED MAP OS Explorer 329 Lowther Hills, Sanquhar & Leadhills

START/FINISH Grid reference: NX 873129

DOG FRIENDLINESS Keep on lead near livestock

PARKING Museum of Lead Mining car park

PUBLIC TOILETS At car park

A unique combination of changing pressures within the earth's crust several million years ago, led to the formation of rich mineral veins in this part of the Southern Uplands. Everything from gold to zinc and copper has been found locally, but it was the rich deposits of lead that resulted in the establishment of Scotland's highest village. By the 17th century a permanent, if primitive, settlement was established. Accommodation consisted of one-room cottages with often as many as eight people living in them. They cooked over the open fire in the middle of the room and smoke was vented through a hole in the roof.

By the late 19th century, when lead mining was at its peak, some 850 people lived here in much improved cottages. These cottages were bigger, with an attic room and a proper cooking range. In 1871 the miners founded a co-operative society, bought all their supplies there and received a share of the profits. Amazingly this continued until 1971.

A Thriving Community

The miners valued the little leisure time they had and were very active in forming local clubs and societies. There were curling, bowling and quoiting clubs, a drama group and even a silver band. The Library, the second oldest subscription library in Europe, was founded in 1756 by the minister and a small group of villagers. Wanlockhead fared better than most libraries with a donation of books from the local landowner the Duke of Buccleuch. He also funded the building of a new school and the salary of the teacher.

The miners' children learned to read, write and count and could also take lessons in Latin and Greek. A government inspector visiting in 1842 was so impressed by the standard of learning he concluded that 'the children of the poor labourers of Wanlockhead are under as good, or perhaps better system of intellectual culture than even the middle class children of South Britain generally'.

As the price of lead slumped, and mines became exhausted, the miners gradually drifted away. The last of the mines, Glencrieff, closed in 1934 and the village went into decline until only 30 people remained. In the 1960s

WANLOCKHEAD

the local authority offered to re-house them elsewhere but they resolutely refused to leave. Thanks to their determination, an influx of new blood, renovation of houses and the opening of the Museum of Lead Mining, Wanlockhead has survived as a community into the 21st century. But it almost vanished, like countless other mining villages, which are now just names on the map, a few ruins and half-forgotten tales.

WALK 8 DIRECTIONS

1 With the museum to your back turn left and join the Southern Upland Way. Head uphill on steps then, at the top, cross to a stone building with a large white door. Turn right on to a rough road, cross the main road and take the public footpath to Enterkine Pass. Follow this to the front of a white house.

2 Turn left on to the course of an old railway line. Follow this, cross a road then go through a long cutting to reach a fence. Go over a stile to get to Glengonnar Station then follow the narrow path that runs along the left side of the railway tracks from here. Eventually the path runs on to a rough road and in the distance you will see two terraced houses.

3 At the point where telephone wires intersect the road, turn left at the pole on the left-hand side and follow the line of the fence down to some sheep pens. Turn right at the end of the pens and walk out to the main road.

4 Turn right then almost immediately left on to a hill road. Walk uphill on this until the road bears sharp right and a dirt track forks off to the left. Turn left on to the track and keep on it until you reach a gate. Cross over, then veer

left on to a faint track. Follow the track downhill to the point where it comes close to the corner of a fence on your left.

5 Cross the fence and go straight ahead on a faint track, picking your way through the heather. Eventually, as the track begins to look more like a path, you will reach a fork. Go to the right here and cross the flank of the hill passing through some disused tips.

6 The path at this point is little more than a series of sheep tracks and may disappear altogether, but that is not a problem. Ahead of you is a large conical spoil heap and, provided you keep heading towards it, you know you will be going in the right direction.

7 Towards the end of the hill the track heads left, starts to make its way downhill, then passes behind a row of cottages. Veer right, downhill, after the cottages to join the road. Turn left and continue past Glencrieff cottages, then turn right, leaving the road and heading downhill again. Cross a bridge and climb up on to the Southern Upland Way. Turn left along it and follow this back to the car park.

Leadhills Library

In the footsteps of some very literate gold and lead miners.
See map and information panel for Walk 8

DISTANCE *7.25 miles (11.7km)*	MINIMUM TIME *6hrs*	
ASCENT/GRADIENT *755ft (230m)* ▲▲▲	LEVEL OF DIFFICULTY +++	

WALK 9 DIRECTIONS
(Walk 8 option)

At Point ③ on Walk 8, follow the north track towards Leadhills, passing a terrace of two houses on the right, then a short row of cottages before the track terminates at a junction with a narrow road. Turn left and walk downhill towards Leadhills church. At the junction with the Main Street, turn right. Leadhills is the second highest village in Scotland after Wanlockhead and exists for the same reason. Rich in minerals it had always been attractive to prospectors. Gold was once found in abundance around here and was used in the Scottish crown, the oldest royal crown in Europe.

Pass the Hopetoun Arms hotel and then the Leadhills Library, the first public subscription library in Europe. In the churchyard is the grave of John Taylor, who lived to the age 137. An obelisk in front of his grave commemorates William Symington, an early pioneer of steam navigation. Continue along the Main Street, go through a crossroads then pass a turning on the left on to a dirt road just before a clump of trees. After the trees are some cottages and then a rough road. Turn left on to this rough road, go through a gate, pass a water treatment works, through another gate then continue to a third gate in front of some spoil heaps. Go through this then turn right and follow a faint track beside the fence. Climb over an old gate then strike uphill at an angle of 45 degrees.

Although the sheep tracks here are faint or non-existent you will eventually intersect a prominent cut in the hillside, Point Ⓐ. Drop into the cut, turn left and head uphill. At the end of the cut keep going to intersect a hill road. All around this part of the landscape you can see the spoil heaps, quarries and disused mine shafts left by the defunct lead mining industry which has now become a source of great interest for industrial archaeologists.

Turn left and follow the road as it curves right and uphill. On the right is a disused shaft and beyond it an old mine. At a fork in the road go left, then through a gate and head downhill looking for the two huge golf ball radars on Lowther Hill ahead and to the left. Go through the next gate, shortly afterwards the road turns sharp left. From the bend another road branches off to the right (Point Ⓑ), to rejoin Walk 8.

The Battle of Glentrool – Road to Independence

Forest trails lead to the site of Robert the Bruce's turning point during the bitter Wars of Independence.

DISTANCE 5 miles (8km)	MINIMUM TIME 2hrs
ASCENT/GRADIENT 300ft (91m) ▲▲▲	LEVEL OF DIFFICULTY ✦✦✦

PATHS Forest trails, metalled roads, 1 stile

LANDSCAPE Hillside, loch and woodland

SUGGESTED MAP OS Explorer 318 Galloway Forest Park North

START/FINISH Grid reference: NX 396791

DOG FRIENDLINESS Great walk for dogs

PARKING Caldons

PUBLIC TOILETS Caldons Campsite

WALK 10 DIRECTIONS

The year 1314 is etched deep in the Scottish consciousness with Robert the Bruce's famous victory over the English forces at Bannockburn regarded as the culmination of the Wars of Independence. But Bannockburn was not the end of the conflict and it could be argued that an earlier skirmish, when the two nations clashed at Glentrool, was a far more important step on the road to independence.

In the early 14th century Robert the Bruce was advancing his claim to the Scottish throne. He murdered his rival claimant, John, the Red Comyn, in Greyfriars' Church, in Dumfries and launched a series of attacks on the English in the south-west. He was crowned King of Scots at Scone on 25 March, 1306, but following a series of defeats he fled to Rathlin Island, off the Antrim coast, where he regrouped before returning to Scotland early in 1307. After attacking English forces in Galloway, an army was dispatched

to capture him. But this wild and inhospitable part of Scotland was Bruce's home territory and he set up an ambush. Using a small part of his force to lure the English on to the southern shores of Loch Trool, he concealed the bulk of his men on the slopes above the loch. The English were forced to dismount and follow in single file and, when they were at their most vulnerable, the Scots blocked the path and hurled a barrage of heavy boulders down on them. This was the turning point in Bruce's fortunes and he went from here to further victories against the enemy, culminating in the Battle of Bannockburn.

WHERE TO EAT AND DRINK

Eating places are few and far between, but there is no place better for a picnic and you'll find lots of suitable spots on the walk. The nearest tea room is a few miles back on the road to Glentrool at the Stroan Bridge visitor centre. With friendly staff serving a variety of snacks, light meals and delicious hot soup, it's a popular place to stop.

GLENTROOL

Edward I then counterattacked between 1317 and 1319, seizing Berwick, a town of great strategic importance on the border. In 1322 the Scottish nobility appealed to the Pope to support independence in the Declaration of Arbroath. Support was granted in 1324 and in 1328 England finally recognised Scotland as an independent nation in the Treaty of Edinburgh.

Leave the car park and follow the Southern Upland Way markers. Cross the bridge over the Water of Trool. Cross another bridge over the Caldons Burn. Next, take a left turn on to a footpath that runs along the banks of the river. Cross over a bridge.

WHAT TO LOOK OUT FOR

From the south side of Loch Trool look across the water to see the famous Bruce's Stone on its vantage point on the far bank. Behind that is the massive backdrop of Merrick, at 2,765ft (843m) the highest hill in the Southern Uplands with the lower Benyellary in front and to the left, connected by the narrow ridge of the Neive of the Spit. A path to the summit of both starts from near Bruce's Stone (see Walk 11).

Follow this well-waymarked trail and at a fork by a waymarker turn right, and then head uphill and into the forest.

Keep on the path uphill and through a clearing, then go through a kissing gate and re-enter the woodland. Continue along the southern side of Loch Trool until you reach an interpretation board near the loch end. This marks the famous spot where Robert the Bruce and his army cleverly lured the superior English forces into a well-planned ambush and routed the enemy.

Follow the path from here, leaving the woodland and heading downhill and to the left, before leaving the Southern Upland Way. Turn left, go through two gates and over a wooden bridge. Cross the bridge over Gairland Burn and continue. Eventually reaching the bridge over the Buchan Burn, cross over and take the path to the left, branching off uphill.

Follow this to the top and Bruce's Stone, which was raised to commemorate the victory at the Battle of Glentrool, the first victory in the Independence Wars. From here, looking across the clear waters of the loch to the tree-clad hills opposite, is one of the finest views in Scotland. Follow the track past the stone then turn left on to the narrow road. Head through the car park and keep going until you reach a waymarker on the left which leads to a forest trail, and take this to return to the start of the walk.

Cycling on the Merrick

*Follow in the cycle tracks of Davie Bell,
the original mountain biker.*

DISTANCE *9 miles (14.5km)* **MINIMUM TIME** *5hrs*

ASCENT/GRADIENT *2,339ft (713m)* ▲▲▲ **LEVEL OF DIFFICULTY** +++

PATHS *Hill tracks, section to Loch Enoch can be very boggy, 1 stile*

LANDSCAPE *Hills, lochs and trees*

SUGGESTED MAP *OS Explorer 318 Galloway Forest North*

START/FINISH *Grid reference: NX 415804*

DOG FRIENDLINESS *Keep on lead at lambing time and near livestock*

PARKING *Bruce's Stone car park*

PUBLIC TOILETS *At car park*

A 1940s photograph shows a group of young men gathered round the cairn at the summit of the Merrick, south-west Scotland's highest mountain. Nothing unusual there, except for the fact that they all have bicycles. It's a record of the successful outcome of a challenge from a newspaper editor and a tribute to one of Ayrshire's cycling pioneers.

The Highwayman

David E T Bell (1907–65) was born and educated in Dumfries, then moved to Ayr where he worked as a gardener. Health and fitness were his passions and when he was introduced to cycling he saw it as a means to achieve both. But Davie Bell was much more than a sportsman. He was a local historian and an outdoor man with an eye for nature. He had a wonderfully descriptive writing style, which ensured that thousands followed his adventures as 'The Highwayman' in his weekly column in the *Ayrshire Post*.

One week the *Post* published a letter from a reader who had gone to the summit of Merrick on a pony. He closed his correspondence with the challenge, 'It only remains for someone to make the ascent on a bicycle'. The Highwayman rose to the bait and, with four friends, set off through the mist-covered Minnoch Valley heading for Merrick. Riding and walking, sometimes using a sling to carry their bikes, they progressed slowly up the hill, some of them collapsing and gasping for breath, while Davie's pal, Harry Fairbairn kept up a constant monologue, 'Jings this is smashing. I never saw anything like this'. Eventually they reached the summit. Then followed the descent of the sloping ridge of the Neive of the Spit to Benyellary. From Benyellary they covered another 2,000ft (610m) at a slower pace to finally descend through granite boulders to Loch Trool.

Davie Bell's passion for 'rough stuff' continued for the rest of his life, making journeys to remote bothies like Back Hill of Bush or hauling his bike to the summit of Ailsa Craig. On each journey he took his readers with him, producing a weekly column for 30 years. When he died in 1965 subscriptions poured in from friends and admirers and a memorial cairn was erected at Rowantree Toll on the Straiton–Newton Stewart road.

LOCH ENOCH

Kirshinnoch Burn

783 ▲

6 843 ▲

Loch Enoch

Redstone Rig

770 ▲

Merrick

Neive of the Spit

Grey Man of the Merrick ●

545 ▲

5

552 ▲

Kirn Burn

Benyellary ▲
719

Gloon Burn

487 ▲

Loch Arron

Ewe Rig

4

Murder Hole ●

3

Loch Neldricken

Buchan Burn

Mid Burn

Loch Valley

● Culsharg

493 ▲

Buchan Hill

Rig of the Jarkness

Long Loch of Glenhead

2

Gairland Burn

350 ▲
White Brae

324 ▲

Buchan Bridge

🚻P **1**

● Bruce's Stone

Newton Stewart, Stroan Bridge

Loch Trool

● Glenhead

0 _____ ½ mile
0 _____ 500m

37

WALK 11 DIRECTIONS

❶ From the car park at Bruce's Stone head east along the narrow road, across the Buchan Bridge. Continue a short distance then turn left and go uphill to cross a stile. Follow the path along the wall, then veer right and head uphill to rejoin the wall. Go through a gate and turn right on to a path. Follow this up the valley of the Gairland Burn with Buchan Hill on your left.

WHAT TO LOOK OUT FOR

From the corner of Loch Enoch come back a little way to the south-west, heading towards the summit of Buchan Hill and look for a large outcrop called the Grey Man of the Merrick. It's a well-known landmark and resembles the face of a man.

❷ To your left is the ridge of Buchan Hill and to the right is White Brae, and to the farside of that the Rig of the Jarkness. Do not cross the Gairland but keep going on the path to reach Loch Valley, skirting it to the west and then continue beside the Mid Burn to reach Loch Neldricken.

❸ Head for the far west corner of the loch to find the infamous Murder Hole featured by S R Crockett in his novel *The Raiders* (1894). The story is based on a local legend that unwary travellers were robbed on these hills and their bodies disposed of in the loch.

WHERE TO EAT AND DRINK

The Galloway Hills is a pretty remote area. Not only is a picnic a good idea but by the time you've conquered Merrick you will feel in need of sustenance. Other options include a visit to the Stroan Bridge tea room (see Walk 10) and The House O' Hill at Bargrennan (see Walk 13).

❹ From the Murder Hole head north, crossing a burn and then a wall. Pass to the west of Ewe Rig and tiny Loch Arron and eventually reach the south side of Loch Enoch. Don't worry if the track vanishes or becomes indistinct, just keep heading north and you'll eventually find yourself at the loch.

❺ As you approach Loch Enoch you will see the outline of Mullwarchar beyond it and to the right. When you reach the loch go left and cross another wall. The slope in front of you is the Redstone Rig and although you have 1,000ft (305m) to climb it is not particularly taxing.

❻ From the summit cairn of Merrick head downhill towards a narrow ridge called the Neive of the Spit to reach the summit of Benyellary, the Hill of the Eagle. From here follow the footpath downhill beside a dry-stone wall then turn left and keep going downhill, into the forest, to reach the bothy at Culsharg. From there continue downhill to return to the car park at the start.

WHILE YOU'RE THERE

Take a trip to Whithorn where St Ninian founded his early church, Candida Casa, the White House, towards the end of the 4th century. Once a popular place of pilgrimage, and a thriving community until pilgrimages were banned under pain of death after the Reformation, it is once again receiving attention because of recent archaeological discoveries. You can visit the interpretation centre, the dig and the old priory.

On the Trail of the Wigtown Martyrs

*Visit the memorial to two women drowned
at the stake for their religion.*

DISTANCE 4 miles (6.4km)	**MINIMUM TIME** 3hrs
ASCENT/GRADIENT 98ft (30m) ▲▲▲	**LEVEL OF DIFFICULTY** ✤✤✤

PATHS Roads, old railway tracks and pavements

LANDSCAPE River estuary, pasture and woodland

SUGGESTED MAP OS Explorer 311 Wigtown, Whithorn & The Machars

START/FINISH Grid reference: NX 439547

DOG FRIENDLINESS Keep on lead near livestock

PARKING At Wigtown harbour

PUBLIC TOILETS None en route

On 11 May, 1685, two Wigtown women were dragged out on to the salt marshes near the town and tied to stakes. Eighteen-year-old Margaret Wilson and her companion, Margaret McLaughlan, aged 63, had been sentenced to death for their religious beliefs.

The Killing Times

This was during that period in Scots history known as the 'Killing Times' when the Covenanters were persecuted for their beliefs. They were called Covenanters after a petition signed in Greyfriars churchyard in Edinburgh, in 1638, and thereafter in churches throughout the country. The Covenant reaffirmed the belief of Scottish Presbyterians that there was a special relationship between God, as head of the Church, and the people. This ran contrary to the belief of the Stuart monarchy in the divine right of kings. Charles II sought to control the Church by appointing Episcopalian bishops and ministers. Presbyterian ministers were ousted from their churches, but simply took to the hills with their congregations and held open-air services called conventicles. Troops patrolled the hills and moors and if they came across these illegal meetings, broke them up by taking some worshippers prisoner and killing others on the spot.

Sentenced to Death

Margaret Wilson and Margaret McLaughlan were two Wigtownshire Covenanters who were tried in the tollbooth at Wigtown for rebellion and taking part in several battles against the Crown. Found guilty, they were sentenced to death by drowning and taken to the tidal Bladnoch River. When they reached the execution site, the soldiers placed the older woman's stake further out in the estuary so that she would die first and thus terrify her younger companion to the point where she would yield and swear an oath to the King. But this was to no avail. While Margaret McLaughlan drowned the younger woman sang the 25th Psalm and then, as the water started to rise around her, began to pray out loud. The water covered her but after a while the soldiers pulled her up, revived her and

asked her if she would pray for the King. A friend cried out to her urging her to say 'God save the King', but all she uttered was 'God save him if he will, for it is his salvation I desire'. On hearing this some of her relatives urged the commanding officer to release her. He asked her to swear the oath or be returned to the water. She refused saying 'I will not, I am one of Christ's children, let me go'. But they would not let her go and she was again thrust under the water until she died.

WALK 12 DIRECTIONS

1 Leave the car park, turn right and head uphill on a narrow country lane called Harbour Road. The house on the left near the top of the road was the former station house for Wigtown. Just before it you will see a farm gate on the left. Go through it and on to a farm track.

2 Follow the track to the point where it goes through another gate then veer right and climb up the old railway embankment. This has a good grassy surface along its entire length. Proceed along the length of the embankment.

3 A wall across the track will stop you at the point where the former railway bridge carried the track across the River Bladnoch. Turn right and go down the side of the embankment and cross a gate into a field. Veer right and head across the field to the far corner then go through a gate on to the main road.

4 Turn left and walk through the hamlet of Bladnoch. At the junction by a roundabout, cross the road to enter the Bladnoch Distillery car park. After visiting the distillery head back out of the car park and turn left at the roundabout. Continue along this road (the B7005) for approximately 1 mile (1.6km) until you get to a crossroads.

WHILE YOU'RE THERE

Don't miss a visit to the Bookshop in North Mains Street. It has the largest stock of second-hand books in Scotland, displayed in a Georgian building that is a labyrinth of rooms crammed with floor-to-ceiling bookshelves. Comfortable seats can be found in odd corners and by the fire where browsers can sit and, well, browse. The coffee is always on and always fresh. And it's free.

5 Turn right on to the B733 and walk along it to reach Wigtown. When you reach the centre of the town bear left round the square and head towards the large and impressive former county buildings. Pass them on your right, then the church and war memorial on your left and continue downhill. Eventually turn right into the car park for the Martyrs' Memorial.

WHAT TO LOOK OUT FOR

The salt marshes along the last section of the walk are rich in plant and animal life. Look for eel grass, the only flowering plant that can grow under the sea, and glasswort which used to be burned and its ashes used in glass production. You may spot curlews wading in the marshes using their long curved beaks to probe the mud for the tiny invertebrates that inhabit the creeks and pools.

6 Walk through the car park and then turn right and head along the path leading to the Martyrs' Memorial. Turn left and walk out over the sands on a specially constructed wooden causeway to reach the poignant memorial erected on the spot where the two women were drowned.

WHERE TO EAT AND DRINK

Café Rendezvous is a walker-friendly place that serves first-class food, including home-made soup, salads, sandwiches and a small but tasty selection of main dishes. After a long walk refuel on a massive portion of mouth-watering Irish stew or the Wigtown Bay chowder made from freshly caught local fish. Fresh, high-quality local ingredients, a top chef and friendly staff are the key elements in the success of this family-run establishment. Children are welcome in the dining room.

7 Return to the path and turn left. Go through a kissing gate then another gate, slightly below the level you are walking on and to the left. At the end of the path go through another gate in front of the station house, turn left on to Harbour Road and return to the car park.

The Wells of the Rees

Take this strenuous walk along the Southern Upland Way in search of the past.

DISTANCE 6.25 miles (10.1km)   **MINIMUM TIME** 3hrs 30min

ASCENT/GRADIENT 558ft (170m) ▲▲▲   **LEVEL OF DIFFICULTY** +++

PATHS Forest roads, forest track, very rough ground

LANDSCAPE Hills, forest and loch

SUGGESTED MAP OS Explorer 310 Glenluce & Kirkcowan

START/FINISH Grid reference: NX 260735

DOG FRIENDLINESS Keep on lead near livestock

PARKING Near Derry farm

PUBLIC TOILETS None en route

Sitting 'on the hillside at the back of the sheiling called Kilgallioch' wrote Davie Bell, 'are three dome-shaped structures of great antiquity'. These were the Wells o' the Rees, the rees in question being sheep pens surrounding the wells.

A Determined Effort

Davie Bell, popularly known as 'The Highwayman', rode his bicycle all over the roughest parts of south-west Scotland in the 1930s and '40s and chronicled his exploits in a weekly column in the *Ayrshire Post* (see Walk 11). He was intrigued by the Wells o' the Rees and mounted several expeditions in search of them. Although he came close, time and again he was defeated by thick bracken and an almost featureless landscape. Today, the waymarked Southern Upland Way (SUW) takes walkers to within 100yds (91m) of the wells and a signpost points them out. But when Davie Bell was roaming these moors, often on his bicycle, but sometimes on foot, there were no long distance footpaths or signposts. Many paths and tracks would have criss-crossed the moor but they were the tracks used by herdsmen and farmers to reach their remote steadings.

Davie eventually found the wells after getting directions from the farmer's wife at Kilgallioch. He described them as 'three piles of stones... skilfully constructed, with each well having a canopy and the shape of the whole like that of a beehive'. Made of flat stones and oval in shape they were 'streamlined into the hillside, with a recess over the well for a utensil'. Sixty years later the people are gone but the wells remain.

This part of Galloway was sparsely populated before the forestry came, but when trees replaced sheep, shepherds and their families abandoned their lonely sheilings to ruin and decay. With the opening of the SUW, walkers trudge this wild landscape once again. These latter-day pilgrims, follow in the footsteps of early Christians on their way to Whithorn.

Although locals told Davie Bell the wells were built by the Romans, it seems more likely that they were made for the pilgrims. According to the Revd C H Dick in his *Highways and Byways of Galloway and Carrick*, the wells

WELLS OF THE REES

may have been part of the ancient church and graveyard of Kilgallioch, which was near by, although he walked across the moors from New Luce in 1916 and saw nothing in the way of ruins. The pilgrims' route to Whithorn was also the path followed by lepers on their way from Glenluce Abbey to the leper colony 1.5 miles (2.4km) north of Loch Derry at Libberland.

WALK 13 DIRECTIONS

❶ Cross a cattle grid and head west along the Southern Upland Way (SUW) on a well-surfaced forest road. Pass Loch Derry, on your right in just under a mile (1.6km) and then continue on the forest road, passing a signpost on the left to Linn's Tomb.

❷ Follow the road as it curves to the right, then, following the SUW markerpost, turn left, leave the road and head uphill. It's a steep climb from here, on a well-trodden path with waymarkers.

❸ Cross over a forest road and then continue on the uphill path heading towards the summit of Craig Airie Fell. You'll reach the summit at a trig point.

❹ From the OS triangulation pillar, continue on a well-marked path towards a waymarker on the horizon. Turn left at the waymarker and head downhill on a footpath that twists and turns to another waymarker near the bottom. Turn right here and keep going ahead until you reach the edge of the forest.

❺ The SUW now follows a forest ride. Shortly you'll come to a clearing with a cairn on your left. Keep straight ahead following the

waymarkers to the next clearing where a sign points left to the Wells of the Rees. Turn left and head downhill, across a dry-stone wall and then a gap in another wall. In winter you will find the wells easily but in summer, when the bracken is thick, you'll have to poke about a bit. The first two wells are on your right as you come through the gap and the other is off to the left.

❻ Retrace your steps from here to the signpost and turn left. Continue along the Southern Upland Way to reach a junction with a forest road. Turn left and follow it to the end, then continue along a faint path, cross a wall and continue east towards Craigmoddie Fell.

❼ Climb to the highest point then look to your left to Loch Derry then, to the right of it, Derry farm. Head in a straight line for Derry farm then drop down off the fell and pick up a path heading towards Loch Derry.

❽ Follow this to go through a gate and on to the forest road. Turn right and return to Derry farm and the start.

The Standing Stones of Laggangarn

Prehistoric relic on the pilgrims' route to Whithorn.
See map and information panel for Walk 13

DISTANCE *7.5 miles (12km)*	MINIMUM TIME *4hrs 30min*
ASCENT/GRADIENT *115ft (35m)* ▲▲▲	LEVEL OF DIFFICULTY +++

WALK 14 DIRECTIONS
(Walk 13 option)

From the forest road junction (Point **Ⓐ**), the Southern Upland Way continues straight ahead to a wooden bridge over the Tarf Water. Immediately, cross another forest road, then head uphill to the Standing Stones of Laggangarn. Originally part of a stone circle they have stood here for about 5,000 years and were on the main pilgrims' route from Edinburgh to Whithorn. Those early Christians incised crosses on the stones adopting them for their own purposes. As you stand before them consider that over the centuries countless thousands have stood on this same spot, among them Robert the Bruce and Mary, Queen of Scots.

After the stones the track drops to a clearing at the ruins of Laggangarn and the odd-looking Beehive bothy (Point **Ⓑ**). On this remote patch of moor this offers the only shelter and is a convenient spot for lunch. The next stage of the walk is rough and wet, and in a few years' time may be complicated by clear-felling. So while eating your lunch, consider whether to take the easier option, which is simply to retrace your steps to the forest road junction (Point **Ⓐ**).

Otherwise, continue Walk 14. With the front door of the Beehive to your back, go ahead, passing to left of the Laggangarn ruins. The going gets tough from here as you encounter rough, uneven and often boggy ground. Veer left within the wide tree gap to cross a wire fence, then the Tarf Water, and turn left to follow the line of a ruined wall and the course of the burn upstream. After 0.25 mile (400m) the wall and fence bend away left, and a U-bend in the burn is just ahead. Here turn right along a forest ride. It bends half-left, narrows, and rises to a T-junction where you turn left. Cross the remains of an old wall to emerge into clear-felled ground. Above on the left is the ruined gable-end of the farm of Killgallioch. The Highwayman, Davie Bell, arrived here in the 1940s having cycled over the moors. He was seeking directions for the Wells of the Rees (Walk 13), which were not then conveniently signposted.

Keep ahead with mature trees on your right and the clear fell up on your left, to pass through a wall gap with a clump of willows just beyond it. Here (Point **Ⓒ**) bear slightly right on the faint path of Walk 13.

Castle Kennedy Gardens

*Discover the gardens around the ancient stronghold
of a powerful family.*

WALK 15

DISTANCE 6 miles (9.7km)	**MINIMUM TIME** 3hrs 30min
ASCENT/GRADIENT 49ft (15m) ▲▲▲	**LEVEL OF DIFFICULTY** ✦✦✦

PATHS Estate roads, lanes, minor road and rough paths, 1 stile

LANDSCAPE Estate woodlands, lochside and pastures

SUGGESTED MAP OS Explorer 309 Stranraer & The Rhins

START/FINISH Grid reference: NX 108597

DOG FRIENDLINESS Dogs should be kept on leads

PARKING On-street parking in Castle Kennedy, opposite gardens

PUBLIC TOILETS None en route

WALK 15 DIRECTIONS

This is the ancient parish of Inch, a burgh of Barony since the 17th century and once a major stronghold of the Kennedy family, from which both the ruined castle and the village take their names. The Kennedys of that period were a much feared and powerful family.

Walk towards the A75 Euro Route, cross it and go through the main entrance to Castle Kennedy Gardens. This is part of the Southern Upland Way (SUW) and follows the main drive into the gardens. Go over a crossroads and follow the drive as it turns left and heads along the banks of the White Loch (or Loch of Inch). On the east bank is Lochinch Castle built in the Scottish baronial style in 1867 and the current home of the Earl and Countess of Stair. Continue along the road, following the waymarkers, as the road passes the entrance to Castle Kennedy Gardens, for which there is an admission charge.

Castle Kennedy Gardens were created on 75 acres (30ha) of land around the ruins of Castle Kennedy, which was burnt down in 1716. They were the creation of the 2nd Earl of Stair who, as British Ambassador to France, had been inspired by the grand gardens at Versailles.

The earl had been one of Marlborough's generals in the War of the Spanish Succession (1701–14) and this enabled him to acquire the use of troops from the Inniskilling Fusiliers and Royal Scots Greys to transform the peninsula between the White and Black lochs into the gardens you can see today.

WHERE TO EAT AND DRINK

The Plantings Inn at Castle Kennedy village is a modern pub with a relaxing and pleasant atmosphere. It's a favoured pit stop for many of the countless hundreds of walkers who pass here each year on the Southern Upland Way. The friendly staff serve food all day and the beer on tap is Bellhaven, one of Scotland's finest real ales.

CASTLE KENNEDY

From the entrance bridge to the gardens turn right and head uphill to reach a T-junction. Turn left on to a country lane then take the next left beside a lodge. Follow this estate road through woodland along the banks of the Black Loch (or Loch Crindil). To your left is a small wooded island shown on the maps as Heron Isle. This is a crannog, an artificial island created in prehistoric times as a habitation, which would afford protection from wild animals and marauding tribes. Look out on this stretch for some of the many birds that can be seen near the water's edge. The lochs are a haven for species such as grebes, ducks and geese.

At a junction near the head of the loch turn left and cross a bridge. You will shortly reach a crossroads. Go straight ahead and, at the next crossroads, go right and follow this road until it reaches a T-junction beside another estate lodge.

When the earl was creating his garden he first built a huge, round pond then installed some terraces and had them planted with a variety of botanical specimens. There are avenues flanked by trees grown from seeds, dazzling displays of azaleas, rhododendrons and spectacular embothriums, more commonly known as Chilean fire bushes. A country trail with numbered posts runs through the garden guiding visitors to some of the best parts including the avenue of monkey puzzle trees, which is at least 100 years old.

Leave the estate and turn left on to a country lane and look out for a track on the left about 0.5 mile (800m) along. Turn left, continue along this farm track until it terminates at a T-junction on another estate road and turn right. To your left is a graveyard and the remains of the old church of Inch, which is worthy of a closer look. Behind it is the White Loch, or Loch of Inch, and the small island of Inch Crindil.

The estate road ends at a T-junction beside another lodge. Cross the A75 Euro Route. On the other side pass the modern Inch church and continue along a minor road which runs beside it.

There is a gap in the wall about 100yds (91m) before a railway bridge. Turn left here by a SUW marker and continue on this well-defined footpath which runs through the woods, roughly parallel to the line of the Stranraer to Girvan railway. It eventually reaches a SUW interpretation board on the edge of the village. Continue to the end of the path and, at a junction with the road, go straight ahead. Turn left at the next junction and return to the car park at the start.

Port Logan or Fictional Ronansay?

*A linear coastal route to a fishing village
where everything is not as it seems.*

DISTANCE	2.5 miles (4km)
MINIMUM TIME	2hrs
ASCENT/GRADIENT	492ft (150m) ▲▲▲
LEVEL OF DIFFICULTY	+++
PATHS	Shoreline, country lanes and hill tracks, 1 stile
LANDSCAPE	Hill, pasture and shoreline
SUGGESTED MAP	OS Explorer 309 Stranraer & The Rhins
START/FINISH	Grid reference: NX 097411
DOG FRIENDLINESS	Keep on lead near livestock
PARKING	Public car park on road to Logan Fish Pond
PUBLIC TOILETS	At car park

The couple standing by a building beside the harbour at Port Logan were perplexed. Pointing to a ferry timetable on a notice board on the wall they asked a passing villager, 'Can you really get a ferry from here to Skye?' The local just smiled and pointed to the sign on the building, which declared it to be Ronansay Primary School. 'It's just a set for the television people,' he told them.

Film Location

Like other visitors to this picturesque village, they could be excused for feeling a wee bit confused. If they walked west along the main street and down some steps to the McPhee Stores, they would have seen a thriving village shop, the walls lined with racks of fresh vegetables, crates of lemonade bottles, plastic buckets and spades and the fishing nets beloved of small children on holiday at the seaside. However, the shop was just a façade. Small clues gave the game away, like the advert for the *Oban Times* beside the door and window stickers advertising the *West Highland Free Press*. Port Logan was the television double for the fictional island of Ronansay in the series *Two Thousand Acres of Sky*.

Fictional Ronansay

In the BBC television series, the island of Ronansay is situated just off the coast of Skye and its islanders are trying to attract new blood into their community. To save the village school from closure, they need an influx of two new children. Michelle Collins stars as a young mother, desperate to escape from a seedy, inner city housing estate, who sees the Ronansay advert and decides it's just what she needs. The only problem is that the islanders are looking for a family and Abby, Michelle's character, is a single mother. She talks her best pal, Kenny, played by comedian Paul Kaye, into pretending to be her husband and going to live in Ronansay with her and the kids. The series has now ended but popular repeats on satellite television ensure a steady stream of visitors in search of the well-known Ronansay locations.

Glorious Scenery

In the outdoor scenes, shot in and around Port Logan, the glorious Galloway scenery takes over as the main star. Nearby Portpatrick masqueraded as Skye and other locations include Dunskey Castle, Drummore and Stranraer.

WALK 16

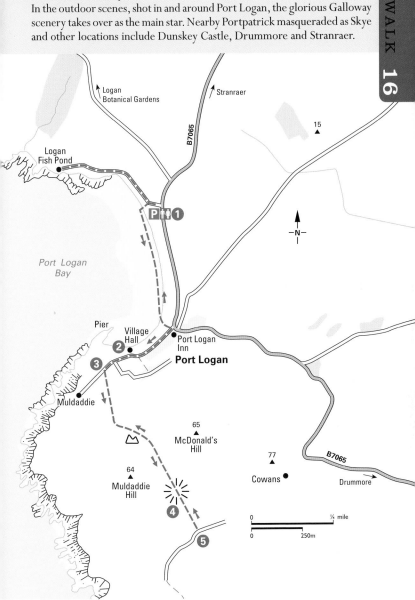

WALK 16 DIRECTIONS

❶ From the car park go across a wooden walkway, down some steps on to the sand and turn left to walk along the beach. When you reach the start of the village, climb on to the road in front of the Port Logan Inn. Turn right and then continue walking along the main street, passing the war memorial to reach the village hall. In *Two Thousand Acres of Sky* the village hall featured as the village school, and had a school sign fixed to the front.

There was also a timetable for Caledonian MacBrayne ferries displayed on a notice board on the wall. Opposite the village hall is a small but picturesque harbour with a rather unusual lighthouse. Nowadays, Port Logan harbour is used only by a few pleasure craft.

2 Port Logan was a thriving fishing port in the past and during the filming of the television series, the pier was festooned with fishing gear, gas bottles and sacks of coal, but they were just props. Move away from the harbour area and continue along the road to the farm of Muldaddie.

3 Just before the farm turn left on to an old hill track and head uphill. Near the top look back downhill for a magnificent view

back to the village and across Port Logan Bay to the Mull of Logan. The track is heavily overgrown here, and is blocked by a barrier made from gates, but this can easily be crossed by a going over a stile at the side.

4 Continue along the track to a T-junction, following the public footpath sign.

5 Retrace your steps to Port Logan then go back on to the beach, turn right and retrace your steps to the car park. From here you can continue along a rough road to the Logan Fish Pond. It's right at the end on the left and is by the only building there.

The Tale of Ardstinchar Castle

The Ayrshire Tragedy, a murder most foul.

DISTANCE 3 miles (4.8km)	**MINIMUM TIME** 2hrs

ASCENT/GRADIENT 295ft (90m) ▲▲▲   **LEVEL OF DIFFICULTY** ✦✦✦

PATHS Country lanes and farm tracks

LANDSCAPE Hillside, pastures and seashore

SUGGESTED MAP OS Explorer 317 Ballantrae, Barr & Barrhill

START/FINISH Grid reference: NX 082824

DOG FRIENDLINESS Mainly farmland, so keep on lead near livestock

PARKING Car park near school on Foreland, Ballantrae

PUBLIC TOILETS Beside car park

If the ruins of Ardstinchar Castle could speak they would tell a tale of a series of events designed to wipe out one branch of Ayrshire's most powerful family, the Kennedys.

Fact or Fiction?

An ancient manuscript lies in a basement in an Edinburgh library. It was written at the time of these events and, although the author remains anonymous, it is believed to be the work of John Mure of Auchindrain House near Ayr. It was the writing of S R Crocket, minister turned novelist, who brought this story to the attention of a wider public when he took it and used it as the basis of his novel *The Grey Man*. This is a work of fiction but woven through the tale is the factual thread of the tragic events which occurred in Ayrshire at the end of the 16th century.

Kennedy Feud

Crocket's novel opens with the fictional burning of Ardstinchar Castle, but he uses this event to outline the origins of the Kennedy feud. This was an attempt by the Earl of Cassillis, the senior Kennedy, to acquire the lands of Crossraguel Abbey. All efforts to persuade Allan Stewart, the Commendator of Crossraguel, failed, so Cassillis seized him, carried him off to his stronghold at Dunure Castle and there in the Black Vault of Dunure 'roasted the hapless Stewart over a slow fire until he signed'. However, Stewart's brother-in-law, Kennedy of Bargany, rescued him and although Cassillis ordered by the High Court to compensate Stewart, he was allowed to keep the lands. Cassillis was thereafter intent on destroying the house of Bargany and plots, intrigues and blood lettings took place, culminating in the murder of Bargany by Cassillis near Maybole in 1601.

Bargany was interred in the family vault at Ballantrae and, although Cassillis escaped justice again, Bargany's ally John Mure, the Grey Man of Crocket's tale, took revenge by having an uncle of Cassillis assassinated. Suspicion immediately fell on Mure but he had an alibi. However, there was one witness who could tie Mure to the crime. A young boy had delivered

BALLANTRAE

a letter from the intended victim to Mure who read it then told the boy to return it and say he had not found Mure. To protect himself, Mure and his son strangled the hapless boy and threw him into the sea near Girvan. The boy's body washed ashore a few days later, both Mures were arrested, tried and found guilty of murder and also of being involved in the assassination. Sentenced to death for their crimes, they were executed at Edinburgh in 1611, thus ending the feud and leaving Cassillis free of any retribution.

WALK 17 DIRECTIONS

❶ Leave the car park and turn left on to the Foreland. At the T-junction with Main Street cross the road and turn right. Near the outskirts of the village, just before the bridge over the River Stinchar, look up to your left to view the ruins of the former stronghold of the Bargany Kennedy's

Ardstinchar Castle. As the castle walls have deteriorated and are considered unstable it is perhaps not advisable to go any closer.

❷ From here cross the Stinchar Bridge and take the first turning on the right, heading uphill on a narrow country lane and past a row of cottages. At a junction in the road keep to the left but

WHERE TO EAT AND DRINK

The Café on the Main Street is a favoured local hang out. It's a cosy wee place, but only open at the weekends. Instead, try the Thistle Tea Room just along the street or the King's Arms Hotel across the road.

look out for one of the Garleffin Standing Stones in the rear garden of the bungalow at the junction.

3 There's another stone in the front garden of this house but you will see that later in the walk. In the meantime continue uphill passing the cemetery, on your right, then Glenapp Castle gates on your left and a little further on the Big Park Civic Amenity Site, on the left.

WHAT TO LOOK OUT FOR

The remaining standing stones of Garleffin formed part of what was a stone circle and it is possible to see the outline by crop marks which are visible from the main Ballantrae to Stranraer road above this hamlet. Local people may tell you that this was once a place of worship for ancient druids but there is no evidence to support that story.

4 The next landmark on the left is the farm road to Bigpark. Continue past this and look out for the next farmhouse on the right. About 300yds (274m) before this house the road dips; there's a stream beside the road here. Turn right on to a farm track that heads downhill between two high hedges.

5 Near the bottom of the hill, just past a large barn on your left, the road splits. Turn right here and continue along this road, through a farm steading, past Downan farmhouse and uphill. When the

road levels out look to the horizon in front of you for the distinctive outline of Knockdolian Hill, often referred to by local mariners as the 'false Craig'.

6 Look over to your left at the same time to see the real Ailsa Craig away to the north-west. Looking along the beach towards Ballantrae is Shellknowe. Continue along this road, past the farm of Kinniegar and through the hamlet of Garleffin. Note that some of the houses have names like Druidslea and Glendruid.

7 In the front garden of Druidslea is another standing stone. Turn left, go downhill on this country lane, turn left on to the main road and return to Ballantrae. Go through a gate on the left-hand side and into the kirkyard. The Kennedy crypt can be found by going up some steps on the right. If the door is locked you can still see inside through a small window on the door. Return to Main Street and turn left, go along the street and take the first turning left past the library. Walk along this street to reach the T-junction and turn left into Foreland and return to the car park where you started.

WHILE YOU'RE THERE

Head along the shore road to Girvan but branch off to the left at Bennane Lea and keep going until you come to a large brick wall built into the rocks to form a cave. This was once home to Snib Scott, a local hermit. His real name was Henry Torbett and he once worked in a bank but for some reason gave it up for a life of solitude. There's a memorial to him, which you will find on the foreshore opposite the cave.

Byne Hill and the Firth of Clyde

Enjoy the views across the sea to Ailsa Craig,
the source of the world's curling stones.

DISTANCE 3.75 miles (6km)	**MINIMUM TIME** 3hrs
ASCENT/GRADIENT 571ft (174m) ▲▲▲	**LEVEL OF DIFFICULTY** ✦✦✦
PATHS Farm roads, dirt tracks and open hillside, 1 stile	
LANDSCAPE Hill, pasture, woodland and seaside	
SUGGESTED MAP OS Explorer 317 Ballantrae, Barr & Barrhill	
START/FINISH Grid reference: NX 187955	
DOG FRIENDLINESS Keep on lead, this is sheep country	
PARKING Ainslie Park car park	
PUBLIC TOILETS At the car park	

The lone sentinel of Ailsa Craig in the Firth of Clyde, which dominates the seaward views on this walk, is the plug of a volcano, extinct since prehistoric times. First mentioned in the charters of the Abbey of Crossraguel in 1404 as the Insula de Ailsay, the island was part of that estate until the Reformation in 1560. Since then it has belonged to the Cassillis family, and has given its name to the senior family member, the Marquis of Ailsa. To generations of immigrant Irish it was known simply as Paddy's Milestone as it is located approximately half-way between Belfast and Glasgow. But Ailsa Craig's main claim to fame is as the source of granite used in the world's supply of curling stones.

The fine micro-granite from Ailsa Craig has been used to make curling stones since the beginning of the 19th century. On the island there are several kinds of granite, Common Ailsa, Blue Hone and Red Hone. All three have been used in curling stone manufacture but the Blue Hone, a finer grained variety, produced the best running surface. Quarrying stopped in 1971 and Welsh granite was substituted. But each stone still had what was known as an Ailsert, a small coaster of Ailsa Craig Blue Hone granite, inserted in the base.

Originally, quarrying on the island was carried out by the Girvan family, who had a lease from the Marquis of Ailsa. They lived in a cottage on the island during the summer months, blasting and extracting the rock for transport back to Girvan harbour and onwards to the curling stone factory in Mauchline. A small railway line was built to carry the rocks to the island pier for loading on to small fishing boats.

During the summer Ailsa Craig was a busy place. As well as the resident lighthouse keepers, the Girvan family and their workforce, there was a constant stream of day-trippers on cruises from Girvan harbour. They could climb to the small ruined castle, take a tour of the lighthouse and wander around the island. Mrs Girvan supplied afternoon teas in a small café. By the 1950s the Girvans had given up quarrying, shut the café and removed their sheep and goats, leaving the rock to the lighthouse keepers and the birds.

BYNE HILL

Kays of Mauchline, the world's only manufacturer of curling stones, started using Welsh Trevor granite to produce their stones with the Ailsert to preserve the smooth running surface. However, in the summer of 2002, Kays removed some 1,500 tons of granite boulders from the old quarries on the island. No blasting or quarrying took place. They simply collected what was already there to avoid disturbing the island's population of seabirds. Now they will be able to make curling stones entirely from Ailsa Craig granite again.

WALK 18 DIRECTIONS

1 From the car park head south along a pavement alongside the A77. Pass a nursing home on the right, then come to a lane on the left past former Shalloch mill.

2 The pavement disappears so continue along the verge for 200yds (183m). Just before it reappears cross a bridge, then turn left and cross the road.

3 Go on to a farm track that runs alongside a burn. Go over a metal gate and turn right. Follow this newly created road which runs behind Woodland Farm and Ardmillan Castle Holiday Park.

There are several metal gates which you go through on the way. Please ensure that you always close them behind you and leave open any that are not closed.

④ Continue on to the saddle between Mains Hill on your right-hand side and Byne Hill on your left, passing the remains of a monument which was erected to the memory of Archibald C B Craufurd of Ardmillan Estate. As the monument is in poor repair keep a safe distance from it. There used to be a plaque on the front, but some years ago this was removed and dumped in the woods below. Turn left through a gap in the wall and head up the side of Byne Hill to reach a prominent commemorative cairn at the summit. From this vantage point there is one of the finest views of the Firth of Clyde. On a clear day you can see the Antrim coast of Northern Ireland, the island of Arran and the Mull of Kintyre to the north and west,

WHILE YOU'RE THERE

Visit Culzean Castle and Country Park a few miles north along the coast road. This Adam masterpiece was built for the Marquis of Ailsa, senior member of the Kennedy family, who gifted it to the nation just after the Second World War. American President Dwight D Eisenhower, was given use of rooms within the castle for life and these rooms are now on view to the public. A display traces his links with the house. Various events are held in the country park.

and, about 8 miles (12.9km) out in the sea, the distinctive outline of Ailsa Craig.

⑤ With the cairn at your back, walk straight ahead. Cross a saddle between the summit and the lower part of the hill, keeping at first to the higher ground then towards the north side of the hill. Descend very carefully and at the bottom, turn left and follow the wall. Continue until you pass a gate then turn right over a stile and cross the field to then go over the gate on to the farm road at Point ③. From here retrace your steps to the start.

WHERE TO EAT AND DRINK

The Southfield Hotel in nearby Girvan serves a full range of snacks and bar meals and has an excellent restaurant menu. Their fish and chips are particularly tasty after a long day out on the hills. The friendly staff of this family-run establishment ensure that everyone gets a warm welcome.

Kilranny Hill and Steading

An extension takes you over rough ground to a ruined and forsaken shepherd's dwelling.
See map and information panel for Walk 18

DISTANCE *4.25 miles (6.8km)*   MINIMUM TIME *3hrs*
ASCENT/GRADIENT *853ft (260m)* ▲▲▲   LEVEL OF DIFFICULTY +++

WALK 19 DIRECTIONS (Walk 18 option)

From the monument continue following the farm track (Point **Ⓐ**) and where it stops keep ahead on a rough path towards a gate. Go through this, turn right to go through another gate, then veer right for 109yds (100m) and go through a third gate. Then strike off from here at a 45 degree angle uphill. As you reach the high ground, a solitary ash tree will be visible ahead to the left. Heading towards this, go through a gate and follow the line of an old wall.

Follow a faint track left from the wall near a burn, keeping the burn on your left and the ash tree ahead. Just beyond the tree, turn left through a gate and head up towards a gap between the hills called the Nick o' the Nawin (Point **Ⓑ**). Go through the Nick and round Kilranny Hill until Pinbain Hill looms ahead. Make towards Pinbain, cross the dry-stone wall at a gate and turn right, following the wall downhill, through a gate then steeply down to the old coach road (Point **Ⓒ**). In the 19th century, this was the main road to Stranraer. Turn right down the road.

Go through two gates and pass the ruin of Kilranny. As late as the 1960s, the families here used candles and oil lamps, while a coal fire was used for warmth and cooking. At sheep-clipping time, the small enclosure beside the sheep pens would be ringed with wooden clipping benches each straddled by a shepherd. It was a lively scene, particularly when the farmer arrived with a welcome crate of beer.

Leave the ruin with its ghosts of long gone herds and head downhill. At a hairpin bend go straight ahead along a farm track. Go through a gate near a waterfall then right on to a farm road heading uphill.

When the road forks, take the right fork uphill. At the next fork go left and follow this road, going through one gate, to its end. Now follow the edge of the woods on your left round a double horseshoe to the Crow Wood. Go through two gates here then head diagonally right across the field and uphill until you reach a wall. Follow this to the corner of the field and cross a burn to two gates at right angles. With the dry-stone wall on your left, go through the gate in front of you. Circle to the left round the foot of Mains Hill to pick up a faint path that eventually joins the farm track near the monument.

Up the Howe of Laggan

The story of a young shepherd's selfless sacrifice.

DISTANCE *8 miles (12.9km)* MINIMUM TIME *4hrs*

ASCENT/GRADIENT *676ft (206m)* ▲▲▲ LEVEL OF DIFFICULTY ✦✦✦

PATHS *Forest roads*

LANDSCAPE *Hill and forest*

SUGGESTED MAP *OS Explorer 317 Ballantrae, Barr & Barrhill*

START/FINISH *Grid reference: NX 287942*

DOG FRIENDLINESS *Sheep everywhere, essential that dogs are kept on leads*

PARKING *Barr Hill Walks car park*

PUBLIC TOILETS *Barr village*

WALK 20 DIRECTIONS

From the car park head back downhill and turn left at the T-junction. Continue along the forest road to the entrance to Changue House. Where the road forks just past here, keep right. To the left, at the fork in the road, is a renovated building that used to be a shepherd's dwelling. This was where the McTaggart family lived just before the First World War. The father and his sons were all noted shepherds in the area.

There was a blizzard raging early on the morning of 11 January, 1913 when Christopher (Kirstie) McTaggart rose. He went off to the hills to check on his flock.

WHERE TO EAT AND DRINK

Try the King's Arms Hotel in the village of Barr. The Hamilton Arms Hotel in Girvan does reasonable pub lunches, but for something a bit more special that won't break the bank try the Southfield Hotel – it's just round the corner from the police station.

Go through a gate and continue for 100yds (91m). At the fork in the road, by fingerposts, go left and downhill beside the Water of Gregg following the blue and yellow waymarkers. Go right through another gate and keep on the forest road. Cross a bridge and continue along the opposite side of Gregg Water.

This was the route that 19-year-old Kirstie trudged along on that morning. Head bowed into the storm he worked his way steadily uphill, his dog by his side. The landscape here was considerably different at the beginning of the 20th century. There were no conifer plantations to provide shelter or to break the force of a wild and bitter wind. The land for miles around was bare hillside broken only by a network of dry-stone walls.

When the path divides near a bridge, go right and follow the red waymarkers and the sign pointing towards Kirstie's Trail. You are now approaching the Howe of Laggan, a wild and lonely valley in

Kirstie's day. Here he expected to find his sheep, sheltering in their pens. Those which may be buried in the snow would have to be dug out. It's not known if he had to rescue any sheep because Kirstie never returned from the Howe of Laggan. Concerned about his missing brother, his twin, Davie, and a couple of friends went up Gregg Water in search of Kirstie.

WHILE YOU'RE THERE

Visit the ruined church at Old Dailly with its Covenanter stones. High on the gable of the church is a plaque dedicated to William Bell Scott, the Pre-Raphaelite painter and poet who lived at Penkill Castle and is buried in the churchyard.

They found him lying by the sheep pens, still alive but in the advanced stages of hypothermia. In vain they attempted to restore the heat to his frozen body but he died 15 minutes after they found him.

At the next junction turn right and then immediately right again on to a footpath. Cross a bridge and go through a small gate to enter the enclosure at Kirstie's Cairn. A picnic table makes this the ideal spot for a pit stop.

Because the weather was dreadful they were unable to bring Kirstie's body home so they left it where it had fallen, near the present cairn. The dog refused to leave his master and stood guard over the body. Next day the storm had abated and a party of 20 or so brought Kirstie back from the Howe of Laggan. At Kirstie's funeral the minister, the Revd John Angus, suggested that the young men of the community raise a memorial to his memory. Kirstie's Cairn was erected a few paces from the spot where he died.

Return via the footbridge and path to the forest road. Turn left then right and follow the yellow waymarkers. The road climbs here for a fair distance with great views along the Howe of Laggan and once on the top you should be able to see the pass of the Nick of the Balloch in the distance.

When the road forks, keep left and uphill. Follow green cycle route waymarkers which are frequent on this section. At the next junction, keep right and continue uphill. Eventually reach the top of the hill and continue on the road down the other side. Yellow waymarkers will reappear although there is a fair distance with no waymarkers. However it is virtually impossible to get lost on this walk. Eventually reach another junction where the red walk branches away to the left. Follow the yellow waymarkers to the right, go through a forestry gate and descend on the road back to the car park.

WHAT TO LOOK OUT FOR

A legend tells of a fight between the Laird of Changue and Auld Nick. Changue was short of cash and sold his soul to the Devil. When it was time to pay up he reneged, placed his Bible in front of him and drew a circle around him with his sword. The Devil let him be. You can see the circle and the Devil's footprints near the end of this walk.

Kirstie's sacrifice is far from unique. These hills are covered with cairns marking the spot where other shepherds died. About 0.5 mile (800m) to the south-west of Kirstie's Cairn, a memorial can be found on the flank of Pinbreck Hill. That was where Kirstie's brother, Jimmy, died many years later.

Discover Dunaskin Ironworks

A hill walk from a 19th-century industrial monument to a deserted, but not forgotten, village.

DISTANCE 4 miles (6.4km)   **MINIMUM TIME** 3hrs

ASCENT/GRADIENT 492ft (150m) ▲▲▲   **LEVEL OF DIFFICULTY** ✦✦✦

PATHS Old rail and tram beds and rough hillside

LANDSCAPE Hill, moorland and industrial buildings

SUGGESTED MAP OS Explorer 327 Cumnock & Dalmellington

START/FINISH Grid reference: NX 440084

DOG FRIENDLINESS Keep on lead near sheep and at lambing time

PARKING Dunaskin Open Air Museum

PUBLIC TOILETS At visitor centre

During the Industrial Revolution, iron was one of the great growth industries. In 1836 Henry Houldsworth, owner of a mill in Glasgow, diversified his business interests and created the Coltness Iron Works. Ten years later he and his son John brought the iron industry to the remote Doon Valley. Henry built his iron foundry on the site of Dunaskin farm and the early Victorian field pattern remains in outline surrounding the works.

New Industry

The area, although rich in iron, coal and water, was almost totally lacking in transport links. Everything for the construction of the foundry had to be brought in by train to Ayr and then by horse to Dunaskin. Twenty-four pairs of horses were needed to haul the great beam for the blast engines alone. Iron was continually produced here from 1848 until 1921, when the buildings became a brickworks and then a processing plant for the coal mines until the late 1970s. One of the most complete Industrial Revolution ironworks in Europe, although restored by a conservation trust and opened as a museum, a lack of funding has resulted in its closure.

At the time the Dunaskin Iron Works were built, the principal industries were agriculture and weaving and the population of the Upper Doon Valley was a mere 250 at Patna and a further 800 in the parish of Dalmellington. Skilled workers were brought in to provide the core of the workforce for the ironworks. They were joined by local men, leaving agricultural work in hope of higher wages, as well as tin miners from Cornwall, itinerant English workers and Highlanders displaced by the Clearances.

New Homes

The company built Waterside village opposite the ironworks to house the large numbers of workers. High above on the Knockkippen plateau, twin villages were built close to the iron ore mines. The twin villages of Lethanhill and Burnfoothill were considered as one, commonly known as the 'Hill, by the close-knit communities. Linked to the outside world by tram and railway lines, this community survived the closure of the mines, the end of smelting at Dunaskin and two world wars. Ironically it was killed off by the post-war drive to improve housing.

Sanitation and overcrowding were a problem on the 'Hill and when the local authority decided to concentrate new building in nearby Patna and Dalmellington, the quality of the new housing and the clean living space it offered was irresistible. No one wanted to leave but gradually the population dwindled until the last man, James Stevenson, departed on 31 August, 1954. All that remains today are the bare outlines of houses among the trees, the war memorial and a simple stone painted white with the poignant inscription 'Long live the Hill 1851–1954'.

WALK 21 DIRECTIONS

❶ Turn right in front of the visitor centre and follow the road towards the adventure playground. Go uphill on a track to the right of the playground and through a kissing gate into woodland. Emerge at a T-junction

opposite a railway bridge and then turn left here on to a grassy trail.

❷ When you reach a metal gate across the trail, go through a small wooden one at its side. Climb over the next gate, turn right and head uphill following the line of a disused tramway, between the ends of an old bridge. This is the trackbed of the former horse-drawn tramway, which was used in order to bring the iron ore down from the plateau.

3 At the top of the hill, when the path divides, keep left and follow the path as it goes through two short sections of wall. The ground to your right in front of the conifer plantation was once the village football field. Where the path is blocked by a fence, turn right and then go left to walk through a gate and right on to a metalled lane.

WHAT TO LOOK OUT FOR

The foundations of the former church and schoolhouse can be seen on the ground behind the war memorial. The church was sold to a local silver band and was rebuilt in Dalmellington. Look also in the remains of the houses of Low Row for floral tributes hung on the trees by former residents who still walk here on a regular basis.

4 Head along here, past the remains of the miners' houses of Step Row, which are clearly visible amongst the trees. A stone memorial to the 'Hill stands near the site of the former village store. To the right of this, and now within the wood, is the former village square and the remains of more houses.

5 From the stone memorial turn back towards the war memorial, then return to the gate at the corner of the wood and continue along the track beside the wood. In the trees are the remains of Low Row. Go through another gate and continue along the former railway. When it forks, keep right.

WHERE TO EAT AND DRINK

The Hollybush Inn on the road to Ayr serves reasonably priced bar meals, including bowls of excellent hot soup. Travelling in the other direction you could try one of the hotels in the centre of Dalmellington.

6 Continue until the route ahead is blocked by sheets of corrugated iron. Cross the wall and turn right, heading downhill to pick up a faint path. Continue on this to reach a cluster of trees beside a ruined building.

7 Head down from here towards the right of a row of cottages. Go through a gate, turn right then right again at a fork to reach Ardoon. Go past the house, turn left on to a footpath and follow it downhill and under a small, disused railway bridge. Cross the track and carry on, heading back downhill on the footpath which leads back to the visitor centre.

WHILE YOU'RE THERE

Don't miss a visit to one of Scotland's most fascinating railway museums. Just along the road, on the north edge of Dalmellington, is the Scottish Industrial Railway Centre, operated by enthusiasts from the Ayrshire Rail Preservation Group. This is as much part of the local story as the ironworks and every Sunday in July and August they offer trips on a working steam train.

On Old Roads and Rails Around Muirkirk

Walk around a once prosperous moorland town that stood at the crossroads of history.

DISTANCE 3.5 miles (5.7km)   MINIMUM TIME 3hrs

ASCENT/GRADIENT 16ft (5m) ▲▲▲   LEVEL OF DIFFICULTY ✦✦✦

PATHS Old railway beds, farm tracks and country lanes, 1 stile

LANDSCAPE Undulating farmland and dense woodland

SUGGESTED MAP OS Explorer 328 Sanquhar & New Cumnock

START/FINISH Grid reference: NX 696265

DOG FRIENDLINESS Good, locals walk their dogs here

PARKING Walkers' car park, Furnace Road

PUBLIC TOILETS None en route

In the early 17th century Muirkirk was not much more than a crude little settlement called Garan on a dirt track that ran from Ayr to Edinburgh. The building of the Moor Kirk of Kyle led eventually to a name change to Muirkirk. An abundance of natural minerals such as coal, limestone and iron ore in the locality would inevitably make it a centre of industry and bring great prosperity.

'Tar' McAdam

Coal mining was well under way when John Loudon McAdam (1756–1836) came here in 1786 to set up a tar works. Known locally as 'Tar' McAdam, he would later go on to develop his famous method of road construction and this is where he carried out his initial experiments. Furnace Road, leading to the walkers' car park, was used in his first trials and road surfaces are still referred to as 'tarmac' today.

Iron and Coal

Muirkirk became the site of Ayrshire's first ironworks in 1787 when James Ewing & Co opened here. Three years later a canal had been dug to transport ore and coal on a series of barges from the Lightshaw, Auldhouseburn and Crossflat mines east of the works. Tram lines ran to the west and a series of bogie tracks led from the various pits to the canals. The Kames Colliery was opened in 1799 and would become the longest operating coal mine in the area. The canal was eventually replaced by the railway when the Glasgow and South Western Railway Company opened the Auckinleck-to-Muirkirk branch line in 1848. From this main line a maze of spur lines ran to the production areas.

Muirkirk became a prosperous, thriving community. It was the first town in Britain to get gas lighting following the construction of the Muirkirk Coke & Gaslight Co in 1859. At its peak, it had a population in excess of 5,000 with 1,000 employed in the ironworks alone.

But nothing lasts forever. Mines become exhausted, or seams run out and industrial trends change. The ironworks ceased production in 1923, following a strike by the workers. Iron ore mining had stopped some time previously and the ore was shipped in from further afield. During the strike the furnaces cooled with iron still inside them and rather than go to the expense of restoring them the company shut down.

The elaborate façade of the industrial works which locals had dubbed 'The Castle' was demolished in 1968, the same year that the Kames Colliery finally closed. By this time the railway had disappeared under the axe of Dr Beeching in the mid-1960s. With no industry left the population drifted away and Muirkirk gradually declined to the small, close-knit community that remains today.

WALK 22 DIRECTIONS

1 From the car park follow the blue waymarker and exit the car park via a gate on to a rough track with a high wall running along to the right. This continues as a fence and, once you are past the end of it, look out for a waymarker pole on your left.

2 Turn left on to a grass track. Follow this to some steps, go downhill and through a kissing gate. Turn right and walk along what may have been the bank of the 18th-century canal.

3 Go through several kissing gates following the River Ayr Way. This recently constructed path runs between two wire fences, along the trackbed, eventually reaching a kissing gate.

4 Go through the gate and turn right on to the quiet country road. Follow this past the remains of an old railway bridge, past a farm entrance on the right then go through a gate to continue on a farm road. At the next gate turn right, go through four gates and return to the car park.

WHERE TO EAT AND DRINK

There is a fish and chip shop in Muirkirk, otherwise try Cumnock, to the west, and enjoy a bar meal in any of the hotels or pubs on the main street or around the town centre.

5 Turn right and exit the car park on to Furnace Road, then turn left. Continue past the clock tower of the derelict Kames Institute and along the edge of a golf course. Go through a gate and continue, passing a cottage on the left, on to the old drove road to Sanquhar. Go through another gate and continue ahead to the McAdam memorial.

6 Just past this head along a green track on the right. Follow this track along the side of a stream until it joins a dirt track

WHILE YOU'RE THERE

Head east on the A70 to the site of the former mining village of Glenbuck. Sadly it has now vanished under a mighty open-cast pit, but it was once the 'Nursery of Scottish Football' turning out a phenomenal number of professional players including the Shankley brothers – the most famous of whom was the legendary Bill who was born here in 1913. A memorial to him stands by the side of the road leading to Glenbuck.

WHAT TO LOOK OUT FOR

No matter where you are on this walk there will be some signs of Muirkirk's former industrial prosperity. Look out for the grassed over beds of former bogie tracks, tramways, railway lines and the outline of the former canal bank. The sandstone building with the clock tower is the former Kames Institute, once an important local social facility and now derelict.

just above Tibbie's Brig. Near here, in a small clay dwelling, lived a local poetess, Tibbie Pagan, who eked out a living by singing, selling her poetry and possibly supplying illicit whisky. She is believed locally to have been the source of the song 'Ca the Yowes tae the Knowes', although Burns himself collected it from a clergyman. In 1803, she published a volume of her collected poems.

7 Go down to the Brig and the monument then return uphill keeping left on the access for the disabled route to McAdam's cairn. Follow this back to the drove road where you turn left to return to the car park.

Darvel's Marvellous Byways

In the footsteps of Sir Alexander Fleming, Darvel's most famous son, and the discovery of penicillin.

WALK 23

DISTANCE *7 miles (11.3km)* MINIMUM TIME *3hrs*

ASCENT/GRADIENT *459ft (140m)* ▲▲▲ LEVEL OF DIFFICULTY +++

PATHS *Country lanes and pavements*

LANDSCAPE *Hillside, moorland, pasture and townscape*

SUGGESTED MAP *OS Explorer 334 East Kilbride, Galston & Darvel*

START/FINISH *Grid reference: NX 563374*

DOG FRIENDLINESS *Dogs on lead in lanes*

PARKING *On-street parking at Hastings Square at start of walk*

PUBLIC TOILETS *None en route*

Lochfield Farm, the birthplace of Alexander Fleming (1881–1955), was the ideal childhood home for a boy with an insatiable curiosity about nature. Together with his brothers, the young Alexander spent much of his time roaming the moors identifying birds, animals and plants and guddling (catching by hand) trout in the nearby burns. He regarded his early education at Loudoun Moor School and later at Darvel as the foundation on which his later career was built.

Medical School

By the age of 13 he had moved to London to live with his brother Tom. Finishing his education at London Polytechnic, Fleming spent four years working as a clerk in a shipping office until the death of an uncle left him a small legacy which enabled him to take a short course of private tuition. He gained first place in the examination which would allow him to enter medical school. Fleming subsequently took first place in every exam he sat. By 1906 he had joined the Inoculation Department at St Mary's Hospital in Paddington and by 1909 was a Fellow of the Royal College of Surgeons. The war interrupted his career at St Mary's but after it he returned there and by 1928 had become Professor of Bacteriology.

A Fortunate Discovery

That year, while clearing up some old virus cultures in his laboratory, Fleming noticed that although all were covered in moulds, one was significantly different. This particular mould was dissolving the virus colonies round about it and was spreading across the dish destroying the rest. The mould was one of a class called penicillium and, as Fleming afterwards stated, 'It was my good fortune that one particular penicillium blew on to a culture plate I was playing with'.

Discovering what we now know as penicillin was just the beginning. Isolating, extracting and finding a means of using it to treat infection would take another ten years and it was the 1940s before this 'magic bullet' was commercially available. Since then it has saved countless lives and a

DARVEL

huge industry has grown round the research and development of other antibiotics. Honours were heaped upon Fleming. In 1944 he was knighted. The following year he was awarded the Nobel Prize for Medicine and on 26 October, 1946, he returned to his native Darvel to receive 'the proudest title I could have… the Freedom of Darvel'. Fleming spent the rest of his life working, lecturing and travelling. His last visit to Darvel was in June 1952 when he presented the Alexander Fleming Dux Medal and addressed the pupils at his old school. On 11 March, 1955, Fleming died from a heart attack; he is buried in St Paul's Cathedral.

WALK 23 DIRECTIONS

1 From the Alexander Fleming Memorial, cross the square to the pedestrian crossing, cross over the road, turn right and go along Main Street. Near the outskirts of the town go across Darvel Bridge and take the second turning on the left just past the John Aird factory.

Go uphill on this road and pass the cemetery on the left.

2 Keep going uphill to reach a crossroads near New Quarterhouse farm. Follow the waymark arrow pointing left. The road continues uphill, passing Henryton on the right and then Byres on the left. Near Byres there

69

is a conveniently situated bench by the roadside if you want some respite on this steep climb.

3 Little Glen is the next farm on the left-hand side and shortly afterwards the road forks. Take the left turn. The next two farms passed on this road are Meikleglen and Feoch which come in quick succession. Just before the next farm on the left, Laigh Braidley, a farm road leads off to the right. This is the entrance to Lochfield, Alexander Fleming's birthplace, which is not open to the public. Continue past Laigh Braidley.

4 After Laigh Braidley the road turns sharply left, then right and goes downhill to cross the Glen Water at Braidley Bridge. As you descend the hill look slightly to the right and uphill and you will see the steading of Lochfield, which is still farmed. Follow the road uphill from the bridge. There's another bench by the roadside at the T-junction near the top of the hill. Enjoy a well-earned rest here and appreciate the splendid view back across the Irvine Valley.

5 Ignore the waymark and turn left, heading along a lane and past Gateside. When the road forks take the left fork, cross Mucks Bridge and continue uphill. The lane now passes the roads to Low then High Carlingcraig, then levels out. As you continue along the top of this hill look to the left for the distinctive outline of Loudoun Hill.

6 When you reach Dyke the road heads downhill again. Go over a crossroads at Intax and continue a short distance to some bungalows on the right. Just past here take a left turn. After Hilltop the road turns sharply right and downhill. As you approach the town the lane continues into Burn Street. At the T-junction turn left and follow this back to Hastings Square.

And on to Newmilns

A longer walk taking in the lace capital of Scotland.
See map and information panel for Walk 23

DISTANCE 11.5 miles (18.5km)   **MINIMUM TIME** 6hrs
ASCENT/GRADIENT 98ft (30m) ▲▲▲   **LEVEL OF DIFFICULTY** ✦✦✦

WALK 24 DIRECTIONS
(Walk 23 option)

The Irvine Valley was a major centre of handloom weaving for centuries. Huguenot and Flemish immigrants fleeing religious persecution in the 16th century brought with them advanced skills including home lace-making and the draw loom for pattern weaving.

At Intax (Point **A**), turn right heading along a country lane passing Cronan on the left and the road to Brownhill on the right. Take a left turn where the road forks. The lane turns sharply right and then left as it passes Dalwhatswood, then continues steeply downhill to enter the town of Newmilns.

By the end of the 18th century, Newmilns had become the centre of the Ayrshire weaving industry. The quality of Irvine Valley weaving was further improved by Joseph Hood, a talented and inspirational engineer and loom builder.

Follow this street to the T-junction then turn left and head along the Main Street. At Criagview Road turn right, go past the library, cross a bridge and turn left on to Brown's Road to Darvel. A short distance along this road, near a lodge house and estate gates, go left on to a footpath and follow it along the banks of the river. The footpath ends near another lodge house and entrance gates to Lanfine Estate. Turn left here and cross Ranoldcoup Bridge. Continue along Ranoldcoup Road, with the park on your left, and look out for the splendid architecture of Darvel Nursery School, also on the left.

At the T-junction, cross Main Street and continue along Cross Street. Turn left at the T-junction and go along West Donnington Street, looking out for the old lace factories, some of which still produce lace today.

Alexander Morton purchased a lace curtain machine and Joseph Hood continued to improve the machinery in the lace factories. But, unable to compete with lace from Nottingham, the Irvine Valley went into decline. However, a revival of interest in traditional cotton lace, has brought new life to Darvel and Newmilns, where some 19th-century looms are still found in operation.

At the junction with Burn Street (Point **B**), turn left and continue back to Hastings Square.

The Museum of Scottish Country Life

An 18th-century time warp in a late 20th-century new town.

DISTANCE *5 miles (8km)*   MINIMUM TIME *3hrs*

ASCENT/GRADIENT *262ft (80m)* ▲▲▲   LEVEL OF DIFFICULTY ✦✦✦

PATHS *Farm tracks and country roads*

LANDSCAPE *Pastureland, woodland and new town*

SUGGESTED MAP *OS Explorer 342 Glasgow*

START/FINISH *Grid reference: NS 608558*

DOG FRIENDLINESS *Keep on lead near livestock*

PARKING *Car park at Museum of Scottish Country Life*

PUBLIC TOILETS *At museum*

On the outskirts of East Kilbride, Scotland's largest and busiest new town, Wester Kittochside farm sits in a time warp. Preserved as the Museum of Scottish Country Life, it is still a working farm but without any of the high-tech machinery of 21st-century farming – its clock has stopped in the 1950s.

John Reid

In 1567 John Reid, the tenant of Kittochside, bought land from Robert Muir of Caldwell. Muir tried to retake the land by force some 20 years later, attacking the farm 'armed with spears, swords and other fearful wapponis'. Reid was threatened, his possessions seized and his house burned. But the matter was adjudicated by the Privy Council, which found for Reid and ordered Muir to pay compensation.

'Modern' Farming Methods

The agrarian revolution to modernise and industrialise farming was enthusiastically embraced in the 1780s by Reid's descendant, another John. He transformed his arable land and his sheep grazed the moorland. New fields were laid out and enclosed, and drainage was installed to improve the ground. Reid introduced crop rotation, new crops, including turnips and grass for winter feed, and changed the stock emphasis to cattle. By the time he was finished, most of the old buildings on the farm had gone, replaced by the new steading that stands today. The Reid family continued to farm at Wester Kittochside. A dairy and barn were built in the latter half of the 19th century and a threshing mill and horse 'gin' (engine – a large wheel turned by horse power to run machinery) were installed.

Time Stands Still

In 1963 dairy production ceased and the land switched to grazing beef cattle. James Reid, the tenth generation to farm here, never carried out any improvements or modernised his farming in any way and for a period of 50 years Wester Kittochside remained completely unchanged. Reid continued to farm as his father had done and he was taught in the 1950s, so no grain driers, huge silos, slurry tanks or modern cattle units were installed.

A Lasting Legacy

James Reid and his wife had no children and gifted the farm to the National Trust for Scotland. James died in 1982 and Margaret, his wife, carried on until 1992 when she left the house ending nearly four centuries' occupation by a single family. Since the farm opened to the public as a museum, the dairy has been reinstated and the land is farmed as it was in 1950, including the five to six shift crop rotation and grazing supporting milk cattle and working horses. Crops of grass, hay and turnips are still used for winter feed. The techniques and equipment evoke memories of a way of life that has long past, except here at Wester Kittochside farm.

WALK 26 DIRECTIONS

❶ Exit the car park and turn right on to the road, heading past the front of the main Exhibition Building then turn right on to a footpath. Continue along this, to reach a T-junction.

② Turn right and follow this to another T-junction with the main road. Turn left and continue along the road, passing the fields and steading of Wester Kittochside.

③ Keep on this quiet road for just over a mile (1.6km), past more of the fields of Wester Kittochside farm, then the fields of more modern farms and finally into the village of Carmunnock. The road ends at a T-junction. Turn right then, a short distance further on, take the next turning on the right into Cathkin Road.

WHERE TO EAT AND DRINK

The museum Exhibition Building contains an excellent child-friendly café where visitors can enjoy hot soup, sandwiches, snacks and sweet things. Alternatively go into East Kilbride and seek out the heart of the old village and try the bar meals in the 18th-century Montgomery Arms, the oldest pub in the area.

④ Keep on Cathkin Road for about 0.5 mile (800m) then, when it bends sharply to the left, turn right and continue straight ahead on a minor road. Follow this as it twists and turns to reach Highflat Farm after about 0.5 mile (800m) and then continues for another

WHILE YOU'RE THERE

The Museum of Scottish Country Life is one of the most important and entertaining attractions to have opened in Scotland for decades. The main Exhibition Building has a comprehensive collection covering the history of Scottish farming. However, it is the farmstead and the magnificent Georgian farmhouse, unchanged in the last half century and little changed since the 18th century, that turns an interesting visit into a magical experience.

0.5 mile (800m) to end at a T-junction opposite the road leading to West Rogerton farm.

⑤ Turn right and, in just over 0.5 mile (800m), you will come to a crossroads. On the right is a farm track leading back to Highflat. Turn left here and proceed to the next T-junction. Walk along this country lane passing the farm of East Kittochside on the left.

WHAT TO LOOK OUT FOR

The fields at Wester Kittochside remain unaltered since the last century, in marked contrast to those of nearby farms. Compare the hedgerows and fields of Wester Kittochside with Highflat to see the differences in fencing and the abundance and variety of wild flowers growing on each.

⑥ Pass a junction on the right, continue through Kittochside, pass the drive to Kittochside House and reach another T-junction. Cross the road and continue along the farm track ahead of you. Take the first turning on the left on to another farm track and, at the end of this, you will then be back in front of the museum Exhibition Building.

The Spectacular Falls at Glenashdale

*Enjoy this short, scenic woodland walk discovering
the Isle of Arran's ancient bedrock.*

DISTANCE 2.75 miles (4.4km)   MINIMUM TIME 2hrs

ASCENT/GRADIENT 442ft (135m) ▲▲▲   LEVEL OF DIFFICULTY ✦✦✦

PATHS Forest paths and forest roads

LANDSCAPE Woodland, waterfalls, rock

SUGGESTED MAP OS Explorer 361 Isle of Arran

START/FINISH Grid reference: NS 047252

DOG FRIENDLINESS Good, locals walk their dogs here

PARKING Car park opposite youth hostel in Whiting Bay

PUBLIC TOILETS None en route; nearest at Shore Road, Whiting Bay

Millions of years ago this area was a hot and barren desert. During what geologists refer to as the Permian period, 270 million years ago, the underlying red sandstone gradually formed from sand dunes. On top of this a sill (layer) of igneous rocks was laid down in the Tertiary period 210 million years later.

The Glenashdale Sill

The Tertiary sill at Glenashdale is about 100ft (30m) thick and composed of several types of igneous rock, the major part being quartz-dolerite. When this is harder than the surrounding rock, it stands proud as the softer rocks are eroded. At Glenashdale continual erosion has created these spectacular waterfalls and, where the stream and the waterfall have cut into the Glenashdale sill, it is easy to examine the now exposed structure of the rocks. Following the stream up from the waterfall, the banks and bed of the stream reveal the dark- and medium-grained igneous rocks with a few specks of pyrites – a shiny yellow mineral. South-west of the falls there are veins of a dark basalt. Pack one of those small geological field guides in your backpack, or in a pocket, and use the photographs to help identify the different kinds of rock found on the route.

Native and Exotic Trees

A field guide to trees could also prove useful although several of the trees have been conveniently labelled. There is an abundance of native trees like the alder, hazel, downy birch, oak, ash and rowan. The latter, also called the mountain ash, has bright red berries in the autumn and in Scottish folklore was used for warding off witches.

You'll also find a wide variety of unusual and exotic trees in the glen. The Siberian crab has white flowers and small green berries which may eventually turn into bright red fruits. You'll also come across large specimens of the Douglas fir. This evergreen native of North America is extensively planted in Europe to provide high grade timber but seldom reaches its maximum height of 328ft (100m). Most European specimens tend to be around 180ft

(55m). Other North American species include the Great fir and the Sitka spruce. This fast-growing conifer often reaches heights of 197ft (60m) and although it thrives in a range of soils, it is particularly suited to the mild, wet Scottish climate.

Growing on the edge of the path you'll find the heart-shaped leaves of wood sorrel with its long-stalked, white, bell-like flowers during April and May. There's a profusion of red campion and the scent of wild honeysuckle and wild garlic mingle with the pine tang of the wood. Look out for the yellow pimpernel, with its star-like flowers, in May and August.

WALK 27 DIRECTIONS

① From the car park turn right on to the road, cross it and turn left on to the footpath, signposted 'Giants' Graves and Glenashdale Falls'. Follow this leafy lane until it reaches the rear of a house, then continue on the path along the river bank. Go through a gate, pass a forest walks sign and then continue until you reach a signpost pointing in the direction of the Giants' Graves.

② The path forks here. Go right, following the sign to Glenashdale Falls. The path continues, rising gently through a wooded area, where several of the trees are identified by small labels fixed to the trunks. Continue uphill on this path, which is marked by the occasional waymarker, crossing a bridge and fording a shallow section of the burn.

❸ Eventually the path starts to climb steeply uphill and continues to some steps and then forks. Keep right and follow this path to reach the falls. Keep on the path past the falls and continue uphill to cross a bridge. A picnic table situated on the river bank here is a good spot to stop for refreshment.

❹ From here follow the path into an area planted with Sitka spruce. Keep to the track marked by the green waymarkers as it heads through this dark part, going through a gap in a wall and eventually arriving at a sign pointing to an Iron Age fort. Turn off to look at the remains of the ramparts then retrace your steps to the sign and continue your route along the path.

❺ Cross over a bridge by another waterfall and then follow more waymarkers to a clearing and a viewpoint. Sit on the bench here and enjoy the panoramic view across the wooded glen. From here you can see the full extent of the impressive Glenashdale Falls as the water cascades over

the top. A waymarker points uphill through a densely wooded area before ending at a T-junction with a forest road.

❻ Turn right on to the forest road and continue, crossing water at a ford and going through three kissing gates until the route continues on a metalled road. Continue along this road, go over a crossroads and wind downhill. Turn right at a T-junction and then walk 200yds (183m) back to the car park at the start.

Machrie Moor

Discover the standing stones of one of Scotland's finest early settlements on the Isle of Arran.

DISTANCE	5.5 miles (8.8km) MINIMUM TIME 3hrs
ASCENT/GRADIENT	114ft (35m) ▲▲▲ LEVEL OF DIFFICULTY ✦✦✦
PATHS	Footpaths, rough tracks, road, 3 stiles
LANDSCAPE	Forest, seashore, fields and moorland
SUGGESTED MAP	OS Explorer 361 Isle of Arran
START/FINISH	Grid reference: NS 898314
DOG FRIENDLINESS	Keep on lead near livestock and where requested by signs
PARKING	King's Cave car park
PUBLIC TOILETS	Car park at Blackwaterfoot

Arran is world famous for its archaeological remains dating from the mesolithic period. The island is littered with them, but the greatest concentration can be found on the wild, windswept Machrie Moor. For it was here that humans settled from the earliest of times and have left the remains of their hut circles, chambered cairns and standing stones. The circles of grey granite boulders and tall, weathered red sandstone pillars are an impressive sight against a winter sun on the wide expanse of moor.

Magnificent Monuments

The earliest inhabitants settled here some 8,000 years ago and, across the millennia, later settlements were created and the first simple monuments erected. Within this small area of moor there are over 40 stone circles, standing stones, chambered tombs and hut circles making it the finest neolithic and Bronze Age site in Scotland. Most visitors head straight for the three large red sandstone pillars, the tallest standing slightly over 18ft (5.5m). These stones were once part of a much larger circle; the other stones have fallen or been removed. No one is certain what function these Bronze Age circles performed, but it is likely that they had a religious significance. Many stone circles are precisely aligned to particular celestial events like the rising of the midsummer sun, and they possibly also fulfilled seasonal functions, indicating when to carry out certain rituals or to plant and harvest crops. A survey of the area by archaeologist John Barnatt in 1978 revealed that four of the circles were aligned with a gap in the skyline of Machrie Glen, where the sun rises at midsummer.

Legendary Figures

Other early Arran inhabitants had another explanation for the circles. At a time when people attributed anything they did not understand to legendary figures, the standing stones on Machrie Moor became the province of the giant Fingal, a Scottish form of the Irish warrior Finn MacCumhail and the double circle still has the name of Fingal's Cauldron Seat. According to legend, Fingal put his dog Bran in the outer circle and tied it to a stone with a hole in it to stop it wandering while Fingal had his meal in the inner circle. The dwellers on the moor lived in round huts, the remains of which are still visible. There is no explanation as to why and when they departed, leaving their monuments, but one theory is that climate change forced them to move to a warmer and more sheltered part of the island. In the thousands of years since they left, the area has become covered by a blanket of peat bog. There is undoubtedly more to discover under this protective layer as recent excavations continue to uncover even older structures.

WALK 28 DIRECTIONS

W A L K 28

① From the car park take the footpath signposted for King's Cave. This goes through an area of woodland, past the site of some hut circles on the right and continues along the edge of the woods until it starts to head downhill towards the sea. Look out for a waymarker on the right pointing back in the direction you have just walked.

② Turn right here on to a faint path, which in the summer will be very overgrown with bracken. Plough your way through this and, in a short distance, you will come to a wire fence, which you can easily climb through. Cross this field and go through a gate, then head downhill aiming for the left end of a white cottage which overlooks the shore.

③ As you near the end of the cottage you will see a gate at the corner of the garden wall. Go through the gate and continue along a farm road running between two fences. Keep on this road passing another cottage on the right and then keeping right when you reach the fork.

④ When the road ends at a T-junction with the A841 turn left. Continue to the signpost for Machrie Moor standing stones. Turn right, go over a stile and follow the access road. This rough track passes through two fields.

⑤ In the second field, near the far left-hand corner, is a megalithic site. Nothing is to be seen above ground, the site was only identified when flints were found that were around 7,000 to 9,000 years old. Continue on the road to the Moss Farm road stone circle from around 2000 BC.

WHILE YOU'RE THERE

A little to the north of Machrie Moor, overlooking Machrie Bay, is Auchagallon Stone Circle. Thought to be a Bronze Age kerbed cairn, it once had a continuous kerb of sandstone blocks around its edge, and is 3,000 to 4,000 years old. Many of the blocks are now missing, but what remains is a stone circle enclosing a burial cairn, the finest burial site on the island.

⑥ From here the track continues, passing the deserted Moss Farm then crossing a stile to the main stone circles of Machrie Moor. When you have finished wandering around them return to the stile and take the Moss Farm road back to the A841. Turn left on to this and walk for approximately 1.5 miles (2.4km) to return to the car park.

WHERE TO EAT AND DRINK

Situated at the edge of the car park at Blackwaterfoot and overlooking the beach, the family-friendly Kinloch Hotel is the best pit stop on this walk. The bar and restaurant meals are of a very high quality and served by friendly staff. Seafood is one of their specialities.

Robert the Bruce

Discover strange geological formations and the cave of a king.
See map and information panel for Walk 28

DISTANCE 5.5 miles (8.8km)   **MINIMUM TIME** 2hrs 30min

ASCENT/GRADIENT 114ft (35m) ▲▲▲   **LEVEL OF DIFFICULTY** ✦✦✦

WALK 29 DIRECTIONS
(Walk 28 option)

From Point ❶ continue past the King's Cave car park and walk a further 2.25 miles (3.6km) to Blackwaterfoot. When the road curves to the left, turn right and head towards Shiskine Golf and Tennis Club (Point Ⓐ). Go through the private car park and past the clubhouse on to a hard surfaced dirt road running parallel to the beach. Follow this as it turns right then forks left to reach gateposts at the drive to Drumadoon farm. Keep left following the signs for King's Cave. Soon another sign points to a path going uphill to the left to King's Cave. Follow this to a gate, cross the stile and continue on a faint path across fields, behind Doon Fort.

This is an Iron Age fort thought to be about 2,000 years old. You can detour to it by following the signs before leaving the golf course.

Go through a kissing gate and continue on the track. Eventually reach a waymarker pointing downhill and follow the narrow twisting track downhill and then left as it continues parallel to the beach through bracken. From here looking back along the beach you have the best view of the sill on Doon Fort. Huge hexagonal columns, like those found on Staffa in west Scotland, or at the Giant's Causeway on the north coast of Northern Ireland, run the full length of the hill.

This well-trodden path continues in this direction to reach the King's Cave (Point Ⓑ). The caves get their name from Robert the Bruce who allegedly hid here for a time during the Scottish Wars of Independence. Whether this is the cave where he encountered the spider is not known, nor is it even certain that he ever did use it. Early humans did though and important archaeological remains have been found there. The caves are fronted by iron bars and kept locked to avoid damage to the interior.

Continue past the caves and follow the shoreline until the path heads uphill on a very steep and badly eroded surface. At the top of this section go over a stile and continue uphill on a rocky path. This will come into the open above the beach (Point ❷). Continue on Walk 28 now or turn right here and keep on this path to return to the car park (Point ❶).

Glasgow's Architecture

*From the heart of the Merchant City to where
it all started in the Old Town.*

DISTANCE *2.5 miles (4km)* **MINIMUM TIME** *3hrs*

ASCENT/GRADIENT *82ft (25m)* ▲▲▲ **LEVEL OF DIFFICULTY** ✦✦✦

PATHS *City pavements*

LANDSCAPE *City streets*

SUGGESTED MAP *AA Street by Street Glasgow*

START/FINISH *Grid reference: NS 592657*

DOG FRIENDLINESS *Not best of walks for dogs*

PARKING *Meters on street bays, multi-story at Buchanan Galleries*

PUBLIC TOILETS *Queen Street Station*

WALK 30 DIRECTIONS

From the tourist office in George Square, turn left into Queen Street and cross the road to the Gallery of Modern Art. This was built as the residence of William Cunninghame, a tobacco lord, in 1778 and is the finest of these mansions in the city. Later it became the Royal Exchange.

Exit the museum and cross to Ingram Street, continuing along past the imposing façade of the Corinthian, formerly the Union Bank and now housing the most ornate pub in the city. Turn right

WHERE TO EAT AND DRINK

Glasgow is the restaurant capital of Scotland and the only difficulty discerning diners have is making a choice. On this walk however its easy, for the Cathedral House Restaurant in Cathedral Square is an absolute gem of a place. French cuisine with a Scottish twist is the order of the day. Try the black pudding salad or the Toulouse sausage on mustard mash.

into Virginia Place and continue through to Virginia Street. Like the rest of the Merchant City, the buildings here were built from the profits from the tobacco and sugar trade. At No 51 is Virginia Court where the tobacco merchants were based from 1817. Later it became the home of Jacobean Corsetry and, although that company has long since departed, their sign has been preserved on the wall. Nos 32–35 were the former Tobacco Exchange then the Sugar Exchange, and are now being converted into apartments. Running parallel to this street is Miller Street where at No 42 is the Tobacco Merchant's House, built in 1775, recently renovated and now housing offices.

From Virginia Street, turn left into Trongate, left into Hutcheson Street, then left again, back into Ingram Street. The white square building with the spire opposite here is Hutchesons' Hall built in 1805 on the site of a previous hospice built by George and Thomas Hutcheson. It now belongs to the National Trust for Scotland. Continue along Ingram Street to

WHILE YOU'RE THERE

The Lighthouse in Mitchell Lane, near Buchanan Street, is one of Europe's largest architecture and design centres and it also contains the Charles Rennie Mackintosh Interpretation Centre. The renovated building, designed by Mackintosh, was previously the home of the *Glasgow Herald* newspaper.

St David's parish church, more often referred to as the Ramshorn Church because of the legend of St Mungo turning a stolen ram's head into stone on this spot. It is now a theatre facility for Strathclyde University.

Continue along Ingram Street then, at the junction, turn left into High Street and proceed uphill. Pass Cathedral Square Gardens on the right, with an equestrian statue of William III, dressed as a Roman emperor. This is 'King Billy' the Dutch-born British monarch still revered by members of the Orange Lodge in Scotland and beyond for defeating the forces of the Stuart kings in the 17th century. The tail of the horse is supposed to move in the wind as it has an ingenious ball and socket joint.

Next to the gardens is the St Mungo Museum of Religious Life and Art. This was built on the site of the medieval Bishop's Castle and exists to promote an understanding and respect of the various religious faiths. Across the High Street from here is Glasgow's oldest house, Provand's Lordship. Built around 1471 for the priest in charge of the St Nicholas Hospital, it later became the house of the Canon of Barlanark, who was rector of the Lordship of Provan. Throughout its long history, the house has had many uses but somehow survived development to become a museum.

Opposite Provand's Lordship is Glasgow Cathedral, a medieval building occupying a site of previous places of worship dating back to the founding of Glasgow, when St Mungo first established his cell beside the Molendinar Burn in the 6th century AD. A fine example of medieval Scottish architecture, it is the only mainland cathedral to have emerged intact from the Reformation. Deep within the building, which is more ornate than its stark exterior would suggest, is the tomb of St Mungo surrounded by four columns supporting fan vaulting. High on a hill behind the cathedral, a statue of John Knox glowers down from his pedestal in Glasgow Necropolis, one of the great 19th-century cemeteries.

WHAT TO LOOK OUT FOR

Just north of the Cathedral Precinct is a pedestrian bridge that goes across the busy road to reach a large, red sandstone school. This is the Martyrs' Public School, a traditional Glasgow public school but with one important difference. This one was designed by Charles Rennie Mackintosh.

From Provand's Lordship, turn left into Cathedral Street. Turn left again at the junction with Montrose Street and then right into George Street and back to George Square. Finish the walk by having a look at the rich ornamentation of the City Chambers, which dominates one end of the square. Built by the Victorian city fathers as a symbol of Glasgow's wealth and prosperity, it is still the municipal headquarters. Its exotic marble interior often moonlights as a film location.

Overleaf: An overview of Glasgow Cathedral, the city's oldest building (Walk 30)

Alexander 'Greek' Thomson

Discover a Victorian city and the architect who shaped it.

DISTANCE **6.5 miles (10.4km)**   MINIMUM TIME **3hrs 30min**

ASCENT/GRADIENT **98ft (30m)** ▲▲▲   LEVEL OF DIFFICULTY **+++**

PATHS *Pavements*

LANDSCAPE *City streets*

SUGGESTED MAP *OS Explorer 342 Glasgow; AA Street by Street*

START/FINISH *Grid reference: NS 587653*

DOG FRIENDLINESS *Not great walk for dogs*

PARKING *Sauchiehall Street multi-storey or on-street parking*

PUBLIC TOILETS *At Central Station*

More than any other architect Alexander Thomson was responsible for the shaping of Glasgow with his innovative use and interpretation of classical Greek designs. Born in 1817, in the Stirlingshire village of Balfron, he moved to Glasgow to live with an older brother. He was apprenticed to an architect and began studying the plans, drawings and engravings of classical architecture. This influence dominated his later style and earned him the nickname 'Greek' Thomson although he never travelled abroad.

Classical Influences

The range of his buildings was extraordinary, from churches to villas, warehouses, tenements and even a set of steps. Much of his work was destroyed by German bombing during the Second World War and even more disappeared in the relentless modernisation of Glasgow during the 1960s and '70s. However, those buildings that have survived provide a fine cross-section of his work. His one remaining church (1857–9) on St Vincent Street is a remarkable building with Grecian columns and an imposing tower, built on the side of Blythswood Hill. Near by, in Union Street, the curiously named Egyptian Halls (1871–3), an enormous stone-fronted building with an interior constructed from cast iron, started life as an early form of shopping centre or bazaar. In the West End, near the Botanic Gardens, Thomson created the Great Western Terrace (1869), the 'grandest terrace in Glasgow' and took the unusual step of placing the tallest buildings in the middle of the row, rather than at the ends, which was more conventional at the time.

Another example of his terraces, Moray Place (1858), is where Thomson took up permanent residence. His home at No 1 is now the contact address for the Alexander Thomson Society and, like most of the houses he designed, is in private ownership. One exception is Holmwood House (1858) in Cathcart, 4.5 miles (7.2km) from the city centre, now owned by the National Trust for Scotland. Built for a wealthy paper manufacturer, it is an asymmetrical villa with a bay window, which looks like a Greek temple attached to the front of the building. It is probably Thomson's finest work.

GLASGOW

Alexander Thomson Society

Although he gained prominence during his lifetime and had a major influence on later architects such as Charles Rennie Mackintosh and Frank Lloyd Wright, Thomson is little known today. Records of his work are limited to a few drawings held in Glasgow's Mitchell Library. His own office archive has vanished without a trace and were it not for the work of the Alexander Thomson Society, he would have remained in obscurity. However after much campaigning to preserve his remaining 24 buildings within the city and the publication of a book about the man, Thomson is beginning to regain the recognition he deserves.

WALK 31 DIRECTIONS

❶ Exit Central Station and turn right. At the junction with Union Street turn right. The building on the opposite corner is the Ca' d'Oro building, a late 19th-century Italianate warehouse by John Honeyman, based on the Golden House in Venice. The upper storeys are made of cast iron. A little way down Union Street from here on the same side as the Ca' d'Oro is Thomson's Egyptian Halls, sadly in need of some renovation.

❷ Cross over then head down Union Street turning left into Argyle Street at the next junction.

Cross Argyle Street, then walk along to the junction with Dunlop Street where you will find the Buck's Head building, named after an inn that previously stood on this spot. Cross Argyle Street again, retrace your steps, turning right into Buchanan Street. Turn left into Mitchell Lane, pass the Lighthouse, then turn right.

❸ Walk up Mitchell Street, continue along West Nile Street then turn left into St Vincent Street. Continue on this for just under 0.5 mile (800m), going uphill to the junction with Pitt Street. You are now standing in front of 'Greek' Thomson's St Vincent Street church, one of his greatest achievements. Cross St Vincent Street here then head up Pitt Street to Sauchiehall Street.

❹ On the opposite corner is Thomson's Grecian Chamber (1865) and to the right along Scott Street is Rennie Mackintosh's Glasgow School of Art. From the front of the Grecian Chamber turn left, head down Sauchiehall Street to Charing Cross, then take the pedestrian bridge over the motorway to Woodlands Road. Go along here until it ends at Park Road, turn right, then left again into Great Western Road.

❺ Go right on Belmont Street, left at Doune Gardens, continue

WHERE TO EAT AND DRINK

The Willow Tearoom in Sauchiehall Street was designed by Charles Rennie Mackintosh for Kate Cranston who had a string of tea rooms. Entered through a jeweller's shop, there is often a queue for the 1904 Room de Luxe, where everything is Mackintosh. It's worth the wait and the food is good and reasonably priced.

WHILE YOU'RE THERE

Thomson designed Holmwood House in Cathcart for James Couper, a paper manufacturer, and everything including the interior design and the furniture came from Thomson's drawing board. Unfortunately the furniture has not survived, but his original paint scheme has been uncovered including a frieze depicting scenes from Homer's *Iliad*. Now in the care of the NTS.

along Doune Quadrant, then left again at Queen Margaret Drive. Cross the road and head down past the Botanic Gardens to turn right, back into Great Western Road. Cross the road and continue to Great Western Terrace, another Thomson masterpiece. Retrace your steps back from here to the top of Byres Road and turn right then, near the bottom, turn left into University Avenue.

WHAT TO LOOK OUT FOR

As you exit the station into Gordon Street the first 'Greek' Thomson building is the former warehouse opposite. Look out for the 'Sixty Steps' as you approach Queen Margaret Drive. There are remains of the former Queen Margaret Bridge on the left behind the former BBC buildings. The 'Steps' used to lead from the bridge to Kelvinside Terrace West.

❻ Go left into Oakfield Avenue, pass Eton Terrace on the corner with Great George Street. Turn right into Great George Street, right at Otago Street, left into Gibson Street and keep going when it becomes Eldon Street. Turn right into Woodlands Road and return to Sauchiehall Street. Follow this to the junction with Renfield Street, turn right and head downhill to Central Station.

The Carbeth Hut Community

*Discover a working-class Utopian dream
near the West Highland Way.*

DISTANCE 3 miles (4.8km)	**MINIMUM TIME** 2hrs 30min
ASCENT/GRADIENT 98ft (30m) ▲▲▲	**LEVEL OF DIFFICULTY** ✦✦✦

PATHS Roads, access tracks and footpaths, 1 stile

LANDSCAPE Hills, woodland and lochs

SUGGESTED MAP OS Explorer 348 Campsie Fells

START/FINISH Grid reference: NX 524791

DOG FRIENDLINESS Suitable for dogs

PARKING Carbeth Inn, check beforehand with landlord

PUBLIC TOILETS None en route

Situated approximately half-way between Glasgow and Drymen on the A809, an old turnpike road, you'll find an ancient inn. Once called the Halfway House and now the Carbeth Inn, it has served the needs of travellers for over 200 years.

Sir Walter Scott had the character of Baillie Nicol Jarvie in his 1817 novel *Rob Roy* describe the inn as a 'most miserable alehouse'. Things have obviously improved since then and for years it has provided a warm welcome to climbers, bikers, walkers and the nearby community of Carbeth hutters.

Holidays in the Country

The Carbeth hut community started after the First World War, when the owner of the Carbeth Estate let three ex-servicemen found a holiday fellowship camp on his land. At first the visitors lived under canvas but during the depression years unemployed Glaswegians, seeking an escape into the countryside, started to erect more permanent dwellings.

These ingenious and often ramshackle affairs were constructed from any materials that were available free of charge or could be obtained cheaply. Conditions were a bit spartan but met the needs of the people and were probably as good as they had at home. During the summers the area round the Carbeth Inn was alive with activity as whole families decamped to the countryside for their holidays.

Peppercorn Rent

The land was leased from estate owner Barnes-Graham at a peppercorn rent, because of his desire to help people escape from what he saw as a squalid and depressing life in the overcrowded city. They became a tight-knit community with organised games and activities; they even built their own open-air swimming pool, complete with lifebelts and diving boards.

To get to Carbeth the hutters caught the train to Milngavie and then took a path which became known as the Khyber Pass. Coming from the Clydebank area the hutters just hoofed it over the Kilpatrick Hills.

CARBETH

Scottish Social History

Today the swimming pool, simply a dammed stream, is silted up. Fashions and lifestyles have changed but Carbeth still has around 200 huts and an active community. A massive increase in the rents led to a rent strike by many of the hutters and court action was initiated to evict them. Against a background of recriminations and accusations, not to mention unsolved arson attacks on huts, the Carbeth community fought to preserve their foothold in the countryside, campaigning for public support and petitioning the Scottish Parliament to preserve this unique piece of Scottish social history and heritage.

WALK 32 DIRECTIONS

1 From the car park at the Carbeth Inn turn right on to the A809. After 0.25 mile (400m) take the first turning right on to the B821. Continue ahead on this road for a mile (1.6km), passing a collection of huts on the left and ignoring a public footpath sign to the right.

2 Turn right at the signpost for the West Highland Way. There's also a Scottish Rights of Way Society signpost beside this pointing to the Khyber Pass Road to Mugdock Country Park. This was the favoured route of the early walkers heading out of Glasgow to the Campsie Fells and beyond.

WHILE YOU'RE THERE

A visit to Mugdock Country Park is a great day out for families. A mere 3 miles (4.8km) from Carbeth it can be accessed by car or as an additional 6-mile (9.7km) round walking trip. In the visitor centre an audio-visual theatre shows a selection of nature videos throughout the day at weekends. There are ranger-led activities, walking and orienteering trails and horse riding can also be arranged at a local stable.

3 Go through a gate and continue along a well-surfaced access road. Ignoring the Khyber Pass turn-off, keep right to follow the West Highland Way along the access road to more huts. After passing the first of the huts and reaching a left bend in the path, look out for a partially concealed public path signpost on the right beside a West Highland Way marker post.

4 Turn right here on to a narrow but well-surfaced footpath and continue along it, passing Carbeth Loch on the right-hand side, to reach the junction with the drive leading to Carbeth House. This is a private house and is not open to the public. Turn left, pass a house and some huts on the right then take the next turning on the left.

5 Continue along this lane, then head uphill to reach another grouping of the Carbeth huts. Follow the main route through the huts and when it forks, keep left.

6 Keep on this road as it passes through the main part of the Carbeth huts, an extraordinary assortment of small dwellings, shanties and shacks. Ignore all of the smaller tracks branching off this road. They allow access to individual huts or other parts of the settlement.

WHAT TO LOOK OUT FOR

If you have the time, and the inclination, look out for a road branching to the left after the first few huts at Point **6**. Having an OS map will help here. This is the road that leads uphill, through a further group of huts, to give access to the top of Carbeth Hill. From this vantage point you will have a grand overview of the entire area and the extent of the hutters encampment.

7 Eventually reach a T-junction. Turn right and follow the lane as it winds downhill to reach the junction with the A809 beside the Carbeth Inn. Turn left and return to the car park.

WHERE TO EAT AND DRINK

Besides being the only option within any distance, the Carbeth Inn is the finest hostelry in this part of Scotland. Retaining its old world ambience, it continues to offer an amazingly varied menu which contains everything from home-made soup, toasties and filled rolls to Scottish favourites like haggis, neeps and tatties and an all-day breakfast which would keep a walker satisfied for many miles. Walkers are very welcome, along with children and dogs.

Glasgow Harbour's Tall Ship

A pleasant walk by the last of the Clyde-built sailing ships.

DISTANCE *4.75 miles (7.7km)*   MINIMUM TIME *3hrs 30min*

ASCENT/GRADIENT *98ft (30m)* ▲▲▲   LEVEL OF DIFFICULTY +++

PATHS *Pavements and footpaths*

LANDSCAPE *Riverside, city blocks, park, botanic gardens*

SUGGESTED MAP *OS Explorer 342 Glasgow; AA Street by Street*

START/FINISH *Grid reference: NS 569652*

DOG FRIENDLINESS *Locals walk dogs on part of route, on lead on busy streets*

PARKING *SECC car park beside Clyde Auditorium (Armadillo)*

PUBLIC TOILETS *SECC*

When she was towed up the Clyde in 1993, the *Glenlee* was a sorry-looking sight. Little more than a derelict hulk, she had been saved from destruction by a group of forward-thinking enthusiasts. Today, restored to her former glory, she is an important part of the regeneration of Glasgow's harbour area.

From Cargo Vessel to Training Ship

Built in 1896 by Anderson Rodger & Co of Port Glasgow, the three-masted steel barque was one of the last sailing vessels launched on the Clyde. She had a long career as a cargo vessel, circumnavigating the globe four times and sailing over a million nautical miles under a British flag. Towards the end of her cargo career, engines were fitted to help keep her on schedule. Three times she ran aground and once almost caught fire, but on each occasion she was rescued. Then in 1921 she became a sail training ship for the Spanish Navy and remained in use until 1981. She sank at Seville, when her sea cocks were stolen to sell as scrap. With her engines drowned and rusted solid it looked like the end.

Lovingly Restored

The Clyde Maritime Trust received a letter from the Spanish Navy giving the ship's details and history and asking if the trust would like to collect the *Glenlee* and save her from being broken up. The trust had very little money but managed to raise enough to purchase, raise her and have her towed back to Scotland. After a short spell in dry dock at Greenock, where an inspection revealed the hull to be sound, she was towed up the Clyde to Yorkhill Quay.

For the next six years volunteers and enthusiasts took on the seemingly impossible task of turning the *Glenlee* back into a sailing ship. The interior cargo holds and accommodation were lovingly re-created. Decking was fitted and Jamie White, a rigging expert from the National Maritime Museum in San Francisco, was called in to restore and reinstall the original rigging. White already looked after the rigging on the *Balclutha*, another

Clyde-built sailing ship, so he knew what he was doing. When work was nearly completed in 1999, the *Glenlee* was towed back down the Clyde to Greenock for the final paint job, known as Gunport, when dark patches were painted on the side to look like gun ports. In days gone by this 'deception' was thought to increase the safety of cargo ships. Old photographs of the *Glenlee* show that she was painted in Gunport at one time.

Fully restored, the *Glenlee* went on public display for the first time when the Tall Ships Race came to Greenock in 1999. Then it was a last tow up the Clyde to her permanent moorings at Yorkhill Quay.

WALK 33

WALK 33 DIRECTIONS

① From the Scottish Exhibition and Conference Centre (SECC) car park go on to the Clyde Walkway and turn right, following signs to the Tall Ship and Museum of Transport (leave the route along here to visit the *Glenlee*). At the roundabout with the Tall Ship on the left, go over a pedestrian bridge to cross the Clydeside Expressway. Go under a bridge into Kelvin Haugh Street.

② Turn west into York Hill Street, then right into Haugh Road and keep ahead, crossing Sauchiehall Street and then along Kelvin Way.

③ Pass the recently restored Kelvingrove Art Gallery and Museum on your left. This is Scotland's number one top tourist attraction and is free.

④ Turn right on to the Kelvin Walkway, right again over the second bridge, then turn left at the Memorial to the Highland Light Infantry. Fork left and follow the river bank.

⑤ This eventually goes uphill. Just before you reach the top of the hill look out for a narrow path on the left. Go left here and under a bridge. Turn left at a cycle path sign to Woodside and Milngavie, go over a bridge and past a café/bar then continue walking along the walkway.

⑥ Cross another bridge, go left at a junction, still following the river. Go under a bridge and then go left across a humpback bridge leading to the Botanic Gardens. Head up the steps to reach the gardens. Turn right alongside the Kibble Palace, turn left and follow this drive to the gates and then exit the gardens.

⑦ Cross Great Western Road at the traffic-lights and walk to the end of Byres Road. Cross Dumbarton Road and turn left into Partickridge Street, right into Dunaskin Street, left at a T-junction then right into Ferry Road. Just before a railway bridge turn left on to a footpath. At its junction with Sandyford Street turn right and continue under the bridge and back to the SECC.

The Clyde Walkway

Walk both sides of the Clyde from the Tall Ship to Glasgow Green.
See map and information panel for Walk 33

DISTANCE *5.75 miles (9.2km)*	MINIMUM TIME *2hrs 30min*	
ASCENT/GRADIENT *Negligible* ▲▲▲	LEVEL OF DIFFICULTY ✦✦✦	

WALK 34 DIRECTIONS
(Walk 33 option)

From the SECC car park, cross the Clyde via Bell's Bridge towards the Glasgow Science Centre. At the end of the bridge, veer left towards the BBC building, pass it and continue walking to the road. Look back to the Finnieston Crane – the largest crane in Europe when it was built in 1932 to hoist steam locomotives on board ships. At a roundabout, turn left on to the main road. Follow this road to another roundabout and turn left. Go right along a quiet road through new housing. Turn left at the traffic-lights and then left again and go down a set of steps at the Etap Hotel. Go through a car park beside the Odeon cinema, then turn right along the riverside walkway (Point **A**).

Continue on the walkway, passing the new 'Squigly Bridge'. When the walkway ends, cross a road and continue walking towards a railway bridge. Pass underneath the bridge and, at the next junction, cross at a pedestrian crossing into Carleton Place. At the end of this street continue along a footpath, up some steps, cross the road and continue along the footpath. Go up some steps and turn left on to Commercial Road. Keep following the river to

a suspension bridge (Point **B**). Cross to Glasgow Green and turn left.

This is Glasgow's main outdoor gathering place and was once the site of the Glasgow Fair. The large sandstone building at the centre is the People's Palace, which covers Glasgow's social history. The ornate and colourful brick building near by is the former Templeton's Carpet Factory, modelled on the Doge's Palace in Venice.

At the end of Glasgow Green, continue on the walkway along the banks of the Clyde. On your way back to the Armadillo you will pass a memorial to those who fought with the International Brigade during the Spanish Civil War. The little black statue of a woman with outstretched arms depicts Dolores Ibarruri, La Passionaria, a Spanish communist and freedom fighter, who famously declared, 'Better to die on your feet than live forever on your knees'.

A little further on is the *Waverley*, the last of the ocean-going paddle steamers. Now restored she still takes trippers 'doon the watter' each summer. Finally, just before the Armadillo and the SECC, is the Finnieston Crane.

Kilsyth and the Forth and Clyde Canal

Travel back in time following along the line of an old Roman wall and an 18th-century canal.

WALK 35

DISTANCE *3.5 miles (5.7km)* **MINIMUM TIME** *3hrs*

ASCENT/GRADIENT *344ft (105m)* ▲▲▲ **LEVEL OF DIFFICULTY** ✚✚✚

PATHS *Tow path, farm road, footpath and road*

LANDSCAPE *Canal, pastures, hillside and woodland*

SUGGESTED MAP *OS Explorer 348 Campsie Fells*

START/FINISH *Grid reference: NS 719770*

DOG FRIENDLINESS *Take care near livestock*

PARKING *Car park near old quarry at Kilsyth*

PUBLIC TOILETS *None en route*

WALK 35 DIRECTIONS

Running almost parallel across the central belt of Scotland are two old lines of communication separated in time by some 1,600 years. Despite their antiquity, both have experienced something of a renaissance of interest in recent years.

WHAT TO LOOK OUT FOR

On the summit of Castle Hill are the traces of an Iron Age fort which stood here long before the Romans came to Scotland. All that remain are two low terraces on the north and west slopes. Sometime during the last couple of centuries BC these and other earthen ramparts would have been surrounded by a wooden palisade and a small group would have occupied some wooden huts safe within.

The Forth and Clyde Canal was the first canal built in Scotland and was created for sea-going vessels. Before it was built, ships had nearly 310 miles (498km) to sail, all the way round the coast

of Scotland to get from the west to the east coast. When the canal was completed the journey was reduced to 35 miles (56km). Construction began in 1768 with a team of navvies digging at Grangemouth on the Forth, and 22 years later they finally reached Bowling on the Clyde.

This revolutionary engineering achievement linked Scotland's two great waterways – the Clyde and the Forth. It also substantially reduced the cost of, and therefore considerably increased, trade between the country's two most important cities, Glasgow and Edinburgh. Because it was built for shipping it had very large locks, 39 of them in total, each 60ft (18m) long and 20ft (6m) wide. A further 3-mile (4.8km) branch section was constructed from Maryhill to Port Dundas, in order to take trade right into the heart of Glasgow.

When it was new, the Forth and Clyde Canal boasted the Kelvin Aqueduct, which at 400ft (122m), was the largest structure of its kind then in existence. In 1802 the trials of the *Charlotte Dundas*, the world's first practical steamboat, were conducted along the canal and Scotland's first iron boat, *The Vulcan*, was built for a passenger service on this waterway. It was also the first canal to carry loaded railway wagons and was eventually purchased by the Caledonian Railway in 1868. It continued to operate well into the 20th century and finally closed to navigation on 1 January, 1963. However, a growing interest in the leisure potential of canals has led to a revival of its fortunes and after extensive restoration and the creation of the revolutionary Falkirk Wheel (see While You're There) it is once more open along its entire length.

Leave the car park on to the main road and turn right. Cross the road and turn immediately left on to a road signposted for Twechar and Kirkintilloch. Continue along this road for a short while and, when it turns sharply right, veer off the footpath to the left and on to the tow path of the Forth and Clyde Canal.

Go round a barrier and keep on along the tow path until it rejoins the pavement beside the main road. Take the next turning on the left, cross the canal via a bridge and enter Twechar. Continue on

this road, heading uphill; near the top keep a look out for a sign on the left pointing to the Antonine Wall and Bar Hill.

Take the next turning on the left on to an access road. Continue along here past some houses and continue on a farm track. Go through a gate and uphill. Look back the way you have come for a grand view of the canal as it winds its way towards Glasgow.

When you reach the entrance to the Antonine Wall go left through a kissing gate and along a grassy lane, then go through another kissing gate to access the site. Veer left and uphill to Bar Hill Fort. From the top of the fort you will see some woodland in front of you. Head for an opening in the trees and then on to a well-defined trail.

Follow this trail through the trees, then up on to the summit of Castle Hill. From here head downhill with the remains of the Romans' Antonine Wall on your left-hand side. Turn right when your path is blocked by a dry-stone wall and follow it until you intersect a farm track.

Turn left and follow this through two kissing gates to reach a T-junction with the main road. Turn left and head down the hill. Keep to the right at the roundabout, still heading downhill to reach another T-junction. From here cross over the road and re-enter the car park.

THE WHANGIE

Exploring The Whangie

Through the hidden opening to the training ground of generations of rock climbers.

DISTANCE 2.5 miles (4km)   MINIMUM TIME 3hrs

ASCENT/GRADIENT 515ft (157m) ▲▲▲   LEVEL OF DIFFICULTY ✦✦✦

PATHS Hill tracks and well-trodden footpaths, 2 stiles

LANDSCAPE Hill, woodland and lochs

SUGGESTED MAP OS Explorer 347 Loch Lomond South

START/FINISH Grid reference: NS 511808

DOG FRIENDLINESS Suitable for dogs, but keep on lead near livestock

PARKING Queen's View car park

PUBLIC TOILETS None en route

Queen Victoria stood near the start of this walk for her first view of Loch Lomond. She never ventured further up the hill and so missed the opportunity to explore the Whangie, a strange cleft in the rock that has fascinated generations of rock climbers.

A Gash in the Rock

Geologists would have us believe that this gash in the rocks, 50ft (15m) deep and 300ft (91m) long, was caused by a landslide, when the surface layer of black basalt moved slowly over the underlying sandstone. This created stresses within the basalt, which eventually fractured, producing thin slices of slab. However, ask any local about the Whangie and you will be told the truth. It was created by the Devil himself on his way to a witches' coven near Stockie Muir. He got so excited that he gave one flick of his mighty tail and carved a slice out of the hillside creating the Whangie. 'Whang' is a common Lowland Scots dialect word meaning 'a slice'.

Early Pioneers

Whatever its origin, the Whangie is still a valued training ground for Glasgow rock climbers, successors to the mountaineering pioneers of the 1920s and '30s. These working-class men from Glasgow started walking out of the city to explore the surrounding countryside. Clad only in their ordinary clothes and with little in the way of equipment, save perhaps some army surplus kit or an old clothes line, they went looking for adventure.

After a hard week of work they would leave Glasgow late at night, take the last bus to the outskirts and walk into the countryside. They had no tents and found shelter where they could, under a hedge, behind a dry-stone wall or in a cave. Some of the great names in Scottish climbing were among these early pioneers, including W H Murray, the celebrated Himalayan climber and environmentalist, and Tom Weir, who climbed with Murray and went on to make a series of television programmes called *Weir's Way*. Weir continued to write a monthly column of his outdoor adventures in *The Scots Magazine* until his late 80s.

THE WHANGIE

Escaping the Slums

From Glasgow they would head to Milngavie and a campfire near Craigallion Loch. Some, like the legendary Jock Nimlin, were fortunate to have friends who possessed huts at Carbeth (see Walk 32), not far from Craigallion and from there they would walk out, 'up the pipe', to Loch Katrine in the Trossachs. They explored all the glorious countryside they could see from the hills around the Whangie – Ben Lomond, the Kilpatrick Hills and the Arrochar Alps. During prolonged periods of unemployment in the depression years these hardy climbers and others like them took to the hills every week to escape the slums of Glasgow. Some even walked all the way to the Highlands.

WALK 36 DIRECTIONS

① Head towards the left of the car park on to the small hillock where Queen Victoria stood for her first breathtaking view of Loch Lomond. Descend and cross a stile over the wall where a well-defined path crosses duckboards and meanders uphill. Turn right to follow the edge of a wood. After the duckboards this is a pleasant grassy walk.

② As you get to the top, near a fence, stop for a while to admire the view. Look away to your right for the expanse of Loch Lomond, Ben Lomond towering over it to the right and the Arrochar Hills away to the left. Cross a ladder stile by a tumbledown fence and turn right on to a narrow but well-trodden path. Follow this along the side of the hill.

3 When the path forks, go left and head uphill. As you near the top you will see the Ordnance Survey pillar on the summit of Auchineden Hill. Head towards this on a clear path. The ground round here is often boggy and you may have to leave the path to bypass the worst bits. To the south from here are the Kilpatrick Hills and, beyond them, the River Clyde. Look for Burncrooks Reservoir to your right and Kilmannan Reservoir to your left. Beyond that is Cochno Loch, another reservoir and a favourite excursion for the residents of nearby Clydebank.

4 Looking towards Ben Lomond, the area in front of you is the Stockie Muir, where the Devil was heading for the tryst that created

WHILE YOU'RE THERE
Summerlee Heritage Park is based in an old ironworks at Coatbridge, east of Glasgow. The history of steel and heavy engineering is what's on offer here in Scotland's noisiest museum. Local engineers demonstrate daily the workings of the historic machines and are busy making spares to restore others. There's a reconstructed tinsmith's shop, brass foundry and spade shop plus rides on an old tramcar along some re-laid track.

the Whangie. Walk towards the Ben on a path leading away from the Ordnance Survey pillar and then go downhill into a dip. Another path runs across this. Turn left on to it and follow it round the side of a small hill. Where the path curves right, look for crags on the right.

5 This is where you'll find the hidden opening to the Whangie. It's easy to miss so look out for a spot on the right where it is simple to climb a few steps up to the crags. It's as if the wall opens up in front of you. Climb into the Whangie and walk to the other end on a path.

6 Exit the Whangie and head to the right on another footpath. Continue on this until it rejoins the path you took on the uphill journey. Go back to the stile, then retrace your steps downhill and back to the car park.

WHERE TO EAT AND DRINK
The superb Carbeth Inn (see Walk 32) is the nearest eating place, a mile (1.6km) south of the car park on the A809. Here you will find a warm welcome for walkers, a wonderful ambience, real ales and everything from home-made soup and sandwiches to snacks and main meals.

WHAT TO LOOK OUT FOR
A variety of wild plants and flowers can be found on this walk. Look for several types of fern on the way. At the Whangie look for wood sorrel with its shamrock-shaped leaves and white flowers with five petals and lilac veins. At the entrance to the chasm are more ferns, heather and red campion, an early summer flower whose blooms open by day to attract butterflies and bees.

Through the Queen Elizabeth Forest Park

*Walking across the Highland Boundary Fault
and along a 19th-century inclined railway.*

DISTANCE *4 miles (6.4km)*   **MINIMUM TIME** *3hrs*

ASCENT/GRADIENT *446ft (136m)* ▲▲▲   **LEVEL OF DIFFICULTY** ✦✦✦

PATHS *Forest roads and footpaths*

LANDSCAPE *Forest and hills*

SUGGESTED MAP *OS Explorer 365 The Trossachs*

START/FINISH *Grid reference: NN 519014*

DOG FRIENDLINESS *Suitable for well-behaved dogs*

PARKING *At visitor centre near Aberfoyle*

PUBLIC TOILETS *At visitor centre*

This walk crosses the Highland Boundary Fault, a geological line stretching across the country from Arran to Stonehaven just south of Aberdeen. It is one of Britain's most important geological features and it separates the Highlands from the Lowlands. This weak line in the crust of the earth formed around 390 million years ago when the old rocks of the Highlands were forced up and the Lowland rocks pushed down. North of the fault lie Highland rocks, created over 500 million years ago when land movement on a massive scale squeezed and heated the stone.

Whinstone, which was used extensively as a building stone because it splits easily, formed from pressure on mud and sand. Slate was also formed but was compressed into layers and was valued as a roofing material.

Slate Quarry

Near the walk is the Duke's Pass, one of the largest slate quarries in Scotland. Most of the higher mountains are formed from a rock known as Leny Gritt, which started life as sand and gravel before being moulded into shape by intense heat and pressure. Another group of rocks includes Achray Sandstone, formed when this high mountain area was under the sea. Later earth movement caused the sandstone to tip and stand on its end. Iron minerals present in the formation of the sandstone gave it a reddish brown colour.

Inclined Railway

Given the quality and variety of the rocks found in this part of the forest park it is unsurprising that in the past a great deal of quarrying took place here. Evidence of a once thriving quarry can be found on the steep downhill path (Point ❹ in the Directions), which, at the beginning of the 19th century, was an inclined railway transporting the limestone from Lime Craig Quarry. The limestone was carried on wooden wagons to the lime kilns which used to be at the bottom of the hill.

Heavy wooden sleepers supported the three rails of the wagon way. Full wagons went down using the centre and one outside rail while the empties returned on the centre and other outside rail. The wagons were attached to a wire rope, which was wound round a drum at the top of the hill enabling the weight of the full wagons and gravity to provide the power to return the empty ones to the top. Halfway up the track was a short section of double railing to allow the wagons to pass each other. Brakes at the top of the incline could be used to control the rate of descent. By 1850 the quarry was exhausted and the wagon way no longer needed.

WALK 37 DIRECTIONS

① From the front of the visitor centre turn left, go down some steps on to a well-surfaced footpath and turn left to follow the blue waymarkers of the Highland Boundary Fault Trail. Continue on this trail to reach the Waterfall of the Little Fawn with

its 55ft (16.7m) drop. Shortly after this turn left to cross a bridge, then turn right following the white arrow left again on to a forest road.

② This is part of the National Cycle Network (NCN) so look out for cyclists. Head uphill on this waymarked road following the blue Highland Boundary Fault markers and the NCN Route 7 signs. When the road forks at a junction, keep left continuing uphill until you reach a crossroads.

❸ Turn right, at the blue waymarker, on to a smaller and rougher road. The Boundary Fault Trail parts company with the NCN Route 7 at this point. The going is easy along this fairly level section. Keep on until you eventually reach a viewpoint on the right with a strategically placed seat.

❹ From here the road heads uphill until it reaches a waymarker near a path heading uphill towards a mast. Turn right then go through a barrier and start descending. Although this is a well-made path it is nevertheless a very steep descent through the woods and great care should be taken.

> **WHILE YOU'RE THERE**
> Blair Drummond Safari Park, on the road between Doune and Stirling, is a good day out for the whole family and the only wildlife park in Scotland. Here you'll see animals ranging from lions and elephants to camels and bison, roaming free. Other park attractions include a pet farm, pedal boats and a waterfowl cruise.

❺ This path follows the line of the Limecraigs Railway, an early 19th-century inclined railway used for transporting limestone. It continues downhill to go through another barrier where the path is intersected by a forest road. Cross this road, go through another barrier and once again continue to head downhill.

❻ At the bottom of the hill is a set of steps leading to a forest

> **WHERE TO EAT AND DRINK**
> The visitor centre at the Queen Elizabeth Forest Park contains an excellent restaurant where you can enjoy a bowl of hot soup, various hot and cold drinks and a host of other delights ranging from sandwiches to hot meals. As an accompaniment to the food you can enjoy some spectacular views over the forest park.

road. Turn right on to the road and follow the blue waymarkers. Stay on this road until you reach a green signpost on the left pointing to the visitor centre. Turn left on to a downhill track and head through the woods.

❼ Eventually you'll reach a board announcing the end of the trail. From here the route is signed back to the visitor centre. When the trail forks take the right-hand turning and head uphill beside a handrail and return to the start.

> **WHAT TO LOOK OUT FOR**
> The surrounding forest is made up of species such as Sitka spruce, Douglas fir, oak, Scots pine, larch, birch and Norway spruce. In January 1968 a gale destroyed large areas of the woodland and the opportunity was taken to clear and replant. Around these areas are more mature plantings from the 1930s and later ones from the 1980s.

The Great Forest of Loch Ard

One of Scotland's great woodlands, hiding place of the
Stone of Destiny and birthplace of the Scottish Parliament.

DISTANCE *3.5 miles (5.7km)*   MINIMUM TIME *2hrs*

ASCENT/GRADIENT *98ft (30m)* ▲▲▲   LEVEL OF DIFFICULTY ✚✚✚

PATHS *Roads, forest roads and trails*

LANDSCAPE *Fields, hills, forest and loch*

SUGGESTED MAP *OS Explorer 365 The Trossachs*

START/FINISH *Grid reference: NS 521009*

DOG FRIENDLINESS *Keep under control or on lead to avoid disturbing wildlife*

PARKING *Car park at Aberfoyle beside tourist office in centre of town*

PUBLIC TOILETS *Beside tourist office next to car park*

Lying between Aberfoyle and the foothills of Ben Lomond, this area of woodland is part of the Queen Elizabeth Forest Park. It stretches from just north of Drymen almost to the banks of Loch Katrine. It may look like just another conifer plantation but a walk through any part of it will reveal a surprising variety of landscapes, flora and fauna.

Forestry Management

Most of the forested land was purchased by the Forestry Commission in the early 1930s. It was planted straight away and by the closing years of the century consisted of mature woodland. Ongoing thinning started in the 1950s and areas were felled towards the end of the century. Some 60,000 tons of timber are extracted each year from the park as a whole. With Britain importing about 90 per cent of its timber needs, the increase in harvesting the park's mature trees will help to reduce this figure.

The area south of Lochan Spling was initially planted with Norway spruce, Sitka spruce, larch and Scots pine. Most of the spruce together with some of the larch and pine was felled in the 1980s and replaced with Douglas fir, larch and Sitka spruce. But native broadleaves have been planted too, including 10,000 oak trees to augment the remains of the ancient oak woods that once covered most of the area. Birch and rowan have been regenerating naturally. Part of this area has been left to mature to provide magnificent specimens, the equal of anything in European forests. The entire area is enclosed within a deer fence to let the trees establish.

Wilderness Areas

Wildlife is abundant, including red squirrels and capercaillie. Decaying pines, which have been uprooted in gales or just collapsed, support wood-boring insects and provide a ready food supply for a whole host of birds. There are peat bogs and wilderness areas like the one just south of Duchray water in the old wood of Drumore. Here there are no trails, but amidst this jungle-like habitat can be found blueberry, chickweed, wintergreen, cow-wheat and cowberry. You will probably see some evidence of red and roe

ABERFOYLE

deer. If you're quiet, you may see rare birds like blackcock and woodpecker. Changing attitudes to conservation and forestry management have helped to bring about a gradual reshaping of the forest to provide diverse tree species, a wider range of habitats and an environment rich in wildlife.

Stop at the Covenanters' Inn where the Nationalists, led by John McCormick, met in 1949 to launch a petition, which they called the Second Covenant. The signatories called on the government of the day to give Scotland a devolved parliament. Over 2 million people signed the petition but it was not until the closing years of the 20th century, and after much argument, campaigning and voting, that their wishes were granted.

WALK 38 DIRECTIONS

❶ Leave from the west end of the car park and turn left into Manse Road. Cross a narrow bridge over the River Forth (the river has its source near here although it is more usually associated with Edinburgh) and continue along the grass beside the road until the first junction on the right. Turn right here and head uphill, passing the Covenanters' Inn. A short distance past here you'll find open countryside and the start of the Great Forest of Loch Ard.

2 Head straight on along the forest road, keeping an ear open for heavy timber lorries. During the week this can get fairly busy, as this is a main forestry extraction route, so keep well into the side. After about 0.5 mile (800m) you will reach a staggered crossroads. Continue straight ahead along the forest road until you come to a turning on the right with a yellow waymarker. Turn right here.

WHERE TO EAT AND DRINK

The excellent Forth Inn is reached from the car park. In good weather, meals and refreshments are served on picnic tables at the front of the inn or within the spacious restaurant. Delicious home-made soups are served with fresh crusty bread or you can choose from the full menu and specials board. They also have toys and colouring books to keep children amused.

3 Follow this waymarked trail through the forest almost to the banks of Duchray Water. This rises on the north face of Ben Lomond and joins with the Avondhu from Loch Ard to create the River Forth near Aberfoyle. The path now curves round to the right, continues to descend slightly and then reaches a junction.

4 Turn right and follow the path through the trees to the north banks of Lochan Spling. The path then swings left and, at the end of the Lochan, turns right at a waymarker pole, crosses a small stream and heads slightly uphill.

5 When the path reaches the T-junction, turn left and rejoin the main forest access road continuing along it to the Covenanters' Inn. This takes its name not from the activities of the 17th-century Scottish Presbyterians, who were persecuted by the Stuart monarchy for refusing to give up their faith, but from the subsequent activities of 20th-century Scottish Nationalists.

WHAT TO LOOK OUT FOR

The Trossachs is an area rich in wildlife. Roe deer is the animal you have the best chance of seeing on the walk. However with a bit of luck, and by keeping quiet, you could also happen on to some of the rarer beasties which inhabit these woods and hills. This is the southern limit for the elusive pine marten and some have even been spotted round Loch Ard.

6 Continue past the inn, where a later group of Nationalists temporarily hid Scotland's Stone of Destiny when it was liberated from Westminster Abbey in 1950, and then turn left on to Manse Road at the junction and return back to the start.

WHILE YOU'RE THERE

Visit Doune Castle, 13 miles (20.9km) east of Aberfoyle, built in the 14th century for the Duke of Albany. It was a ruin by the 18th century but has since been restored and now offers a look at what life was like in a medieval royal household. It featured in the film *Monty Python and the Holy Grail* (1974) and more recently the BBC dramatisation of *Ivanhoe*. Although usually associated with Edinburgh, the River Forth actually rises near here where the Duchray Water meets the Avondhu River. It increases in size by the addition of the River Teith near Stirling, then continues its journey to the coast and flows under the Forth Bridges at Queensferry.

And on to the Duchray Estate

Mustering point for Royalist troops and a bolt hole for Rob Roy MacGregor.
See map and information panel for Walk 38

DISTANCE 6 miles (9.7km) **MINIMUM TIME** 3hrs 30min
ASCENT/GRADIENT 164ft (50m) ▲▲▲ **LEVEL OF DIFFICULTY** ✦✦✦

WALK 39 DIRECTIONS
(Walk 38 option)

At the staggered crossroads (Point **A**), leave the main track and turn left on to a narrower one indicated by a fingerpost for 'Lochard Cycle Route'. This is also marked by a blue Forest Enterprise waymarker pole. From here head uphill, go through a gate and continue up the hill. At a fork in the path, take the right-hand turn. Then, ignoring a turning to the right beside another waymarker post, keep walking straight ahead.

The path continues, still climbing steeply uphill, to reach a viewpoint on the right-hand side near the top of the hill. Stop for a minute here and enjoy the panoramic views across to Loch Ard and the forest to the slopes of Ben Venue. A short distance further on there is another viewpoint on the right.

This is part of Duchray Estate, which also gives its name to Duchray Castle, a 16th-century keep built by the Grahams of Downie. This was the mustering point for an army raised in 1653 by William, 9th Earl of Glencairn, to fight for restoration of the Stuart monarchy. He led 4,000 men in open battle against Cromwell's army and won a minor victory, near Aberfoyle, against government forces under the command of Captain Kidd of Stirling Castle. The insurrection was, however, short-lived and was put down by General Monk, who then burned the castle at Duchray. It was rebuilt and is now in private hands and not open to the public.

During another turbulent period in Scotland's past, Duchray provided shelter, on at least one occasion, to Rob Roy MacGregor (1672–1734). This folk hero or bandit, depending on your point of view (see Walk 42), roamed and raided extensively in this area, seizing cattle and capturing rent money. Not surprisingly he was often hotly pursued by the forces of law and order.

From the viewpoint the path starts its journey downhill again and eventually terminates at a T-junction by two stone cottages. Turn right, back on to the wider forest access road, and continue along it until you reach a yellow waymarker, at a turning on the left, on to a narrower path. Turn left to rejoin the main walk at Point **B** around Lochan Spling.

Overleaf: Loch Ard on the route from Aberfoyle to Loch Katrine (Walks 38 and 39)

Up the Doon Hill

A circular walk in the footsteps of Robert Kirk, the minister who believed in fairies.

DISTANCE *2 miles (3.2km)*   MINIMUM TIME *2hrs 30min*

ASCENT/GRADIENT *220ft (67m)* ▲▲▲   LEVEL OF DIFFICULTY ✦✦✦

PATHS *Roads, forest roads and well-surfaced footpaths*

LANDSCAPE *Pastures, hills and woods*

SUGGESTED MAP *OS Explorer 365 The Trossachs*

START/FINISH *Grid reference: NS 521009*

DOG FRIENDLINESS *Suitable for dogs*

PARKING *Car park in Aberfoyle next to tourist office*

PUBLIC TOILETS *Beside tourist office next to car park*

WALK 40 DIRECTIONS

From the west end of the car park exit on to Manse Road and turn left. Immediately cross a narrow bridge over the River Forth and continue along the road to the cemetery. Enter through a pair of ornate metal gates and cross over to the remains of the church.

Standing on either side of the doorway into the church are two heavy iron objects shaped like coffins. These are mort safes and if you try to lift them you will find them almost impossible to move. They were placed over the coffins of the newly deceased and kept there until the bodies were judged as being decomposed. This was for fear of raids by grave robbers. It was at a time when

WHERE TO EAT AND DRINK

The Forth Inn, near the car park, offers a full menu and specials in the restaurant. Delicious home-made soups are served with fresh crusty bread. In good weather you can enjoy your meal outside at the picnic tables.

medical science was advancing and anatomists in the great medical schools of Edinburgh and Glasgow needed a constant supply of fresh cadavers. They were prepared to pay handsomely with no questions asked. The grave robbers were called Burkers after the notorious Burke and Hare, the Edinburgh grave robbers and murderers of the early 19th century.

Walk from here to the rear of the church and look for a carving with what looks like a dagger crossed with a hook. This marks the burial place of one of Kirkton's ministers, the Revd Robert Kirk. But as any local will tell you, the minister is elsewhere, as you will discover.

From here return to the main gate, leave the churchyard and turn left to continue along Manse Road. Go past some houses and pick up the signs pointing to Fairy Hill. Continue along the forest road and don't be surprised if you come across people with teams of huskies and sleds in winter. As you continue through a gate you will see a sign explaining that this

WHAT TO LOOK OUT FOR

Look out on Manse Road for a large oak tree, called the poker tree. This refers to a story in Scott's *Rob Roy* where Baillie Nicol Jarvie enters an Aberfoyle inn in defiance of a warning to keep out. A fight ensues with the inhabitants and the Baillie, finding his sword rusted in the scabbard, grabs a red hot poker from the fire and uses it, setting a Highlander on fire.

is a Husky Training Route. Near the top of the hill there's a sign pointing to the left and the Doon Hill Fairy Trail Circular Walk.

By modern standards the Revd Kirk would be regarded as barking mad but in the 17th century a belief in fairies was not considered strange, even in the local minister. It was the Revd Kirk's daily practice to walk to the top of Doon Hill, known as the fairy knoll and, according to tradition, the home of fairies. The Revd Kirk himself was the seventh son of the minister of Aberfoyle, something in itself believed to endow a person with certain magical powers like second sight.

Follow the steps of the minister by turning left on to a well-surfaced gravel footpath. Follow it uphill, through the trees and up several sets of steps. Eventually reach the summit of the hill, which is covered in trees.

It was here that the Revd Kirk studied the fairy people and found out all about their habits, homes, superstitions, work and food. He talked to anyone who claimed to have met the fairies. When he had collected enough information he wrote a book about them called *The Secret Commonwealth of Elves, Fauns and Fairies*. It was written

in 1691, eventually published in 1815 and is still being studied by folklorists today.

Legend has it that this telling of tales incurred the wrath of the fairy folk, who were displeased by the fact that mortals could now find out all about them. They spirited the minister away and imprisoned him for eternity on Doon Hill. In reality he died of a heart attack in 1692, on the summit of the hill. He was buried in his own churchyard but again tradition has it that the fairies substituted a changeling for the burial and that the Revd Kirk is imprisoned in a tree on the hill.

WHILE YOU'RE THERE

Take the ferry from Port of Menteith and visit Inchmahome, the largest of three islands on Lake of Mentieth. It contains the ruins of the 13th-century priory used by Mary, Queen of Scots to hide from the English in 1547. A walk around the island takes about half an hour.

As you walk around the top of the hill, you will see coloured cloths, scarves, hats and other objects attached to the branches of the trees. These are offerings to the fairies from visitors. Some messages are attached, mostly asking the fairies to use their magic powers to help make various things come about.

Returning from the summit, take the opposite path from the one you came up on. Don't forget to look back as you leave at the tallest and most prominent tree on the hill. That's where the Revd Kirk is supposed to be incarcerated. Leave the hill and follow the path downhill to rejoin the forest road and turn right. Retrace your steps back to the car park.

Overleaf: Red squirrels inhabit the woodland of Doon Hill (Walk 40)

A Trail Through the Sallochy Woods

A gentle stroll by the bonnie banks of Loch Lomond.

DISTANCE 2 miles (3.2km)   MINIMUM TIME 1hr 30min

ASCENT/GRADIENT 131ft (40m) ▲▲▲   LEVEL OF DIFFICULTY +++

PATHS West Highland Way, forest trail and forest road

LANDSCAPE Loch, hills and woodland

SUGGESTED MAP OS Explorer 364 Loch Lomond North

START/FINISH Grid reference: NS 380957

DOG FRIENDLINESS Suitable for dogs

PARKING Sallochy Woods car park

PUBLIC TOILETS None en route

One of Scotland's best-known songs, *The Bonnie Banks of Loch Lomond*, was reputedly written by a soldier of Prince Charles Edward Stuart's army during the Jacobite rising of 1745. During the long, slow retreat from Derby the soldier was captured and taken to Carlisle Castle and it was here that he wrote the song for his love, while languishing in prison awaiting execution. It tells of their joy in each other's company on the banks of Loch Lomond and how she would make the lonely journey home to Scotland by the 'high road'. Meanwhile his soul would be instantly transported at the moment of death back to his beloved loch along the 'low road' of the underworld and reach there before her. It's a poignant song of love and parting and a nostalgic remembrance of a landscape that the soldier will never see again in life.

Loch Lomond

Loch Lomond is the largest freshwater lake in Britain. It is 24 miles (38.6km) long, 5 miles (8km) wide and, at its deepest point is 623ft (190m) deep. Within its banks are approximately 38 islands, some of which are inhabited while others form sanctuaries for birds and wildlife. Most of them are in private ownership and not open to visitors. Inchcailloch is part of the National Nature Reserve and Bucinch and Ceardach are National Trust for Scotland properties. They can be visited and in summer a ferry and mail boat operate a regular passenger service from the boatyard at Balmaha, allowing island exploration and the opportunity to lunch at the Inchmurrin Hotel on Inchmurrin.

Geological Fault

The loch straddles the Highland Boundary Fault, a fracture caused by movement of the earth's crust millions of years ago, and the geological differences between Highland and Lowland Scotland formed at this time are clearly visible from its banks. Here the fault runs from Conic Hill on the south-east shore down through the islands of Inchcailloch, Torrinch, Creinch and Inchmurrin.

LOCH LOMOND

Forest Park

Most visitors rush up the busy A82 along the west side of Loch Lomond, but on the more secluded eastern shore there is a largely unspoilt area of tranquillity and beauty, even in the height of summer. The diverse woods here are part of the Queen Elizabeth Forest Park and contain walking and nature trails and isolated picnic spots. The variety of animals and plants which can be found is staggering. Over a quarter of the plants that flourish in Britain can be found around the loch. You may well spot the rare capercaillie (it's the size of a turkey), ptarmigan or even a golden eagle. On Inchcailloch white fallow deer have been spotted in the past. While on Inchconnacan you might encounter a wallaby. They were transported here from the Australian outback some years ago, by Lady Arran.

WALK 41 DIRECTIONS

❶ From the car park head towards the entrance on to the main road. Go right on to a track beside the starting post to the Sallochy Trail. Cross the road with care and continue along the trail on the other side. Follow red, green and blue waymarkers. At the second junction turn right and follow the green waymarkers.

2 The trail goes through the wood and passes into the ruined 19th-century farm steading of Wester Sallochy which the Forestry Commission has now cleared of trees. Several buildings can be seen and it's worth spending some time investigating these old ruins and trying to imagine life in those times. When you have finished, circle the buildings to the left and follow the well-worn trail until it ends at a T-junction beside a waymarker post. Turn right on to the forest road here.

WHAT TO LOOK OUT FOR

Large oak trees remain from when these woods were used to provide a constant supply of timber. They were under a coppice system of management throughout the 18th and 19th centuries which divided the area into a series of sections or 'hags'. Each hag was felled every 24 years but the best 400 trees would be left another 24 years and eight of these were spared to go on growing.

3 Follow the forest road for about 0.5 mile (800m) to reach a gate just before the junction with the main road. Cross the gate, then cross the main road. Look carefully for a faint path running through the woods to your left.

WHERE TO EAT AND DRINK

Try the tea room of the garden centre on the shores of the loch at Balmaha. Here you'll find friendly service, food that is hot, tasty and nourishing and some dreadfully fattening cakes. Alternatively eat in one of several cafés and restaurants at Loch Lomond Shores where, as well as superb views, you'll find everything to tempt you from snacks to seafood.

WHILE YOU'RE THERE

Head for Loch Lomond Shores, a new gateway visitor attraction situated at Balloch. Within Drumkinnon Tower are viewing galleries and shops as well as two informative shows and a street theatre troupe. Here you can journey with a young otter through some of the myths and legends of the loch, or watch and listen as the scenery becomes the backdrop to the story behind the well-known song.

4 Follow the faint path back towards the loch (if you miss the track then enter the wood at any point and head west towards the loch). When the track intersects with a well-surfaced footpath, turn right. You are now on the West Highland Way. Follow the waymarkers, keeping on the main path and ignoring any subsidiary tracks branching off it.

5 Follow the path uphill through a rocky section and then, as it levels off, through a wood. Eventually the trail passes through the Sallochy Woods car park returning you to the start.

From Balquhidder to Creag an Tuirc

On the trail of the Highland outlaw, Rob Roy, a 'MacGregor despite them', and on to his final resting place.

DISTANCE 2.5 miles (4km)	**MINIMUM TIME** 2hrs
ASCENT/GRADIENT 328ft (100m) ▲▲▲	**LEVEL OF DIFFICULTY** ✦✦✦

PATHS Forest roads and hillside, 2 stiles

LANDSCAPE Hills, loch and woodlands

SUGGESTED MAP OS Explorer 365 The Trossachs

START/FINISH Grid reference: NN 536209

DOG FRIENDLINESS Dogs okay on this route

PARKING At Balquhidder church

PUBLIC TOILETS None en route

The romantic myth of the life of Rob Roy MacGregor was immortalised by Sir Walter Scott in his novel *Rob Roy* (1817).

Prosperous Cattle Dealer

Born in 1671, the third son of Lieutenant Colonel Donald MacGregor of Glengyle, Rob Roy was exceedingly strong, with long arms. Roy, from the Gaelic 'rhuadh', meaning 'red', denoted the colour of his hair. After his marriage to Mary Campbell he acquired land on the east shore of Loch Lomond and rented grazing at Balquhidder. Soon he was a prosperous cattle dealer but an arrangement with the Marquis of Montrose led to his downfall. In 1711 the Marquis gave Rob Roy £1,000 to buy cattle, one of his men absconded with the money and Rob Roy was charged with embezzlement. Failure to answer the court summons led to him being outlawed and a warrant issued for his arrest. Meanwhile Montrose's factor (his agent handling his business affairs), Graham of Killearn, evicted Rob Roy's wife and family from their home at Craigroyston.

To Outlaw

The Earl of Breadalbane gave Rob Roy some land in Glen Dochart, but as an outlaw he was unable to trade as a cattle dealer. Undeterred he turned to sheep and cattle rustling and offering protection. He harried far and wide, lifting cattle and demanding blackmail. His most vicious attacks were always reserved for the Marquis of Montrose, stealing his cattle and lifting his rents. He was even known to give money to a tenant facing eviction and then ambush the factor to steal it back. Twice Rob Roy was captured but both times he managed to escape. Once in a daring escapade, while fording the River Forth and tied to a horse behind his captors, he severed his bonds and plunged into the fast flowing river. His captors were powerless as the current swept him down river.

In 1715 he raised Clan Gregor for the Jacobite rising of the Old Pretender. When it failed, Rob Roy was charged with high treason but again he managed to give his pursuers the slip and retain his freedom. Government forces burnt his house in Glen Dochart, but in 1716 the Duke of Argyll let him build another in Glen Shira.

Pardoned

After years of being a wanted man he finally turned himself in to General Wade in 1725 and was pardoned by the King. His remaining years were spent in his house at Inverlochlarig at the head of Balquhidder Glen. He died there, peacefully, on the 28 December, 1734. His funeral procession came down the 15-mile (24km) glen on New Year's Day 1735, led by the MacGregor piper. His grave is beside the ruined church in front of the present Balquhidder parish church.

WALK 42 DIRECTIONS

❶ The walk starts at the car park at Balquhidder church. From here, walk along a dirt track, go past a shed and turn on to a path on the right-hand side which gives access into the forest. Follow the direction arrows on the green signposts pointing to Creag an Tuirc, along a forest track and heading up the hill.

2 Continue on this obvious trail for about 0.5 mile (800m) and then turn right, alongside a green building, again following the clearly signposted and waymarked route along a forest road. After another 0.5 mile (800m) go through a gate on the right-hand side, go slightly downhill on some stone steps and across a small stream.

3 The path now heads uphill on some stone steps, through old pine trees and on towards the summit of a knoll. Here is a cairn erected by the Clan Maclaren Society in 1987 to commemorate their 25th anniversary. The plaque proclaims that this place is the ancient rallying point of their clan.

4 A seat below the cairn is a grand place to rest after the climb up here. Sit for a while and enjoy the magnificent views over the meandering line of the River Balvag and the length of Loch Voil with the Braes of Balquhidder rising steeply above it. You can see the route that Rob Roy's funeral procession would have taken from Inverlochlarig down to the village itself, and the churchyard where his body lies. From here, retrace your steps back down the hill but before reaching the top of the stone steps on which you came up, take the path to the left signposted 'Forest Walk'. This continues downhill following waymarked poles, down some steps and across a small bridge. The path goes through some bracken, over a small stream and then across a stile. Eventually it will pass through a small wood of young native trees before emerging on to the forest road.

5 Turn left here and retrace your steps back downhill over the stile and then turn left to return to reach the car park. From here enter the churchyard and turn left. Rob Roy's grave is on the left in front of the ruins of a pre-Reformation church.

The Shores of Loch Katrine

Glasgow's water supply in the heart of The Trossachs.

DISTANCE 6.75 miles (10.9km)		**MINIMUM TIME** 4hrs 30min
ASCENT/GRADIENT 420ft (128m) ▲▲▲		**LEVEL OF DIFFICULTY** +++

PATHS Water board roads, hill tracks

LANDSCAPE Hills, woodland, lochs and heather

SUGGESTED MAP OS Explorers 364 Loch Lomond North; 365 The Trossachs

START/FINISH Grid reference: NN 404102 (on Explorer 364)

DOG FRIENDLINESS Keep on lead near loch and livestock

PARKING Car park at Stronachlachar Pier

PUBLIC TOILETS At car park

Loch Katrine takes its name from the Gaelic 'cateran', a Highland robber – a fitting place then for the birthplace of Rob Roy MacGregor, the bandit, who was born at Glengyle at the western end of the loch. This is the heart of MacGregor country and a clan graveyard lies near the head of the loch. Rob Roy's lasting fame is due to a novel of the same name written by Sir Walter Scott and the loch, too, owed its early popularity to one of Scott's poems, *The Lady of the Lake*. First published in 1810, Scott's description of the scenery encouraged tourists to visit The Trossachs. Coleridge and Wordsworth were inspired by its beauty and Queen Victoria enjoyed a sail upon the loch in 1869. But the pure water of the loch was destined to be a crucial element in the growth of Glasgow as well as a rural escape for its citizens.

By the start of the 19th century Glasgow's population of over 80,000 depended for their drinking water on a few public wells. Later, private companies supplied water from large barrels. But the poor quality of the water, combined with dreadful overcrowding and poor sanitation, led to thousands of deaths from cholera in the 1830s and 40s.

By the mid-19th century Glasgow resolved to provide a municipal waterworks and commissioned John Frederick Bateman, an English engineer. Bateman identified Loch Katrine as the best source of water for Glasgow because of the quality of the water, the large catchment area and its remote, rural, location, but it required a massive feat of engineering. Bateman first built a large dam to raise the level of the loch. Then he constructed an aqueduct 26 miles (41.8km) long to transport the water to a huge reservoir at Mugdock, on the outskirts of the city. A further 26 miles (41.8km) of main piping and 46 miles (74km) of distribution pipes were installed to take the water to all quarters of Glasgow.

After three and a half years, it was officially opened by Queen Victoria in 1859. Bateman was mightily impressed by his scheme and told the city fathers that he had left them 'a work which I believe will, with very slight attention, remain perfect for ages, which for the greater part of it, is indestructible as the hills through which it has been carried'.

LOCH KATRINE

Stronachlachar
Pier

P

1

Loch Katrine

Aqueduct
Outlet

Loch
Arklet

B829

Royal
Cottage

2

265 ▲

Obelisk

Shafts

3

278 ▲ Tom Ard

Shafts

4

A

392 ▲

Lochan
Mhaim
nan Carn

324 ▲

Frenich
Farm

Queen Elizabeth
Forest Park

Loch Ard Forest

420 ▲

Loch
Chon

B829

P

508 ▲

Lochan
Beinn Dubh

482 ▲

Shafts

Culligart Burn

Loch
Dhu

Loch Dhu
House

Shaft

B

Aberfoyle,
Trossachs Pier

0   ½ mile
0   1km

Duchray Water

WALK 43 DIRECTIONS

1 From the car park follow the road back towards the B829 and take the second turning on the left. This is an access road for Scottish Water vehicles only. Continue along the access road until you come to a cattle grid with green gateposts at the building known as Royal Cottage. Turn right just before this on to a rough gravel track that heads through some dense bracken.

> ### WHILE YOU'RE THERE
> Head round to The Trossachs Pier and take a trip on the SS *Sir Walter Scott*, the last of the screw-driven steamships in service on Scotland's inland waters. The trip sails via Stronachlachar and passes Royal Cottage, Ellen's Isle, the Factor's Island and Rob Roy's birthplace at Glengyle House.

2 As the path emerges on to open hillside you will see the first of several ventilation shafts and beyond it, on the hill, a strange obelisk. Follow the path along this line. When you reach the obelisk, be sure to look back for a magnificent view over Loch Katrine below and across to the hills with their narrow passes. This is where Rob Roy and his men moved from Loch Katrine to Balquhidder and

beyond, moving cattle or escaping from the forces of law and order. Continue following the line of the ventilation shafts towards a chimney-like structure on top of a hill. Skirt this hill to the right and then continue around its left-hand side, following an obvious forestry track.

3 Follow this well-defined track past another ventilation shaft. Keep left at the shaft. It can be very muddy on this short stretch. Continue on the path until it intersects a forest road by a stream. Cross the road and look for a faint track continuing downhill in the same direction. In summer this path may be difficult to find because it's hidden by bracken. In this case follow the line of the telephone poles. Eventually after working downhill through more woodland the track emerges on to the B829.

4 Turn right here and follow the road. It will eventually emerge from Loch Ard Forest into open countryside. Loch Arklet can be seen on the left; it is now connected to Loch Katrine by an underground pipeline. When the road reaches a T-junction with the Inversnaid road, turn right. When this road forks, turn right again and return to Stronachlachar Pier.

> ### WHERE TO EAT AND DRINK
> This is one of those occasions where a picnic appears to be the only practical option. There are lots of excellent spots on the route to sit down, pour a cup of hot soup from your flask and enjoy your sandwiches while you gaze in awe at the scenery. Alternatively head back into Aberfoyle to the Forth Inn next to the car park there.

And on to Loch Dhu and Loch Chon

An easy and enjoyable walk, mainly on forest roads.
See map and information panel for Walk 43

DISTANCE *6 miles (9.7km)* **MINIMUM TIME** *3hrs*

ASCENT/GRADIENT *33ft (10m)* ▲▲▲ **LEVEL OF DIFFICULTY** ✦✦✦

WALK 44 DIRECTIONS
(Walk 43 option)

Turn left at Point **Ⓐ** and follow the road passing the Loch Chon (Loch of the Dogs) car park. From the car park the road goes inland a short way until it comes to Loch Dhu (the Black Loch). At the south end of this loch there's a road to the right leading to Loch Dhu House.

Both lochs are very picturesque and this easy and enjoyable walk is mainly on forestry roads. At first glance it would appear to have no connection with industrial archaeology but that's the primary function of this walk.

Cross a bridge (Point **Ⓑ**) and when the road reaches a T-junction look straight ahead for the outline of a ventilation shaft. Turn right and go uphill following the road along the banks of Loch Chon. Keep looking up to the left particularly where there are shafts or towers marked on your map. The latter are markers indicating the line of the mains water pipe from Loch Katrine which supplies water to Glasgow, the former are ventilation shafts with large, well-like structures over them, sealed by huge iron grids.

In the 1930s, large numbers of workers, and the unemployed, would use the pipe track as their main route out of Glasgow, following it on foot until they reached The Trossachs. They were hardy pioneering outdoor people who, with little or no equipment would spend the weekend climbing and exploring the hills, sleeping in the open, under a hedge or in what was left of the bothies and shelters that had been thrown up at the time when the pipeline was built.

Follow this road along the banks of the loch, cross a bridge and pass the turn off to Frenich Farm. To your right are more ventilation shafts. These continue in a line across the road marking the route of the pipe all the way to Royal Cottage on the banks of Loch Katrine. It was near Royal Cottage that Queen Victoria opened the sluice gates to start the flow of water to Glasgow in 1859. As you approach the end of the forest road go through a gate to a T-junction with the B829. Turn left and continue to rejoin the main route (Point **Ⓐ**).

Rest and Be Thankful

A steep climb up one of Scotland's most famous military roads.

DISTANCE 4.5 miles (7.2km)   MINIMUM TIME 3hrs

ASCENT/GRADIENT 426ft (130m) ▲▲▲   LEVEL OF DIFFICULTY ✦✦✦

PATHS Forest roads and metalled road, 4 stiles

LANDSCAPE Hills, glen and forest

SUGGESTED MAP OS Explorer 364 Loch Lomond North

START/FINISH Grid reference: NN 230073

DOG FRIENDLINESS Keep on lead near livestock

PARKING Rest and Be Thankful car park

PUBLIC TOILETS None en route

WALK 45 DIRECTIONS

Prior to the 17th century the Highlands of Scotland were a remote area and, for all practical purposes, inaccessible. Rough drove roads or paths followed the line of glens and rivers and most travel was by foot or on horseback. England had roads dating back to the time of the Romans but there were few roads in Scotland and none at all in the Highlands. Continuing political unrest in the Highlands led the government to dispatch General George Wade to Scotland in 1724. He was charged with pacifying the region. Like the Romans, Wade concluded that an intensive programme of road building would allow the rapid deployment of troops and supplies and enable the army to instigate a greater measure of control.

From the marker stone in the car park, commemorating the renovation of this particular stretch of military road, veer left on to a track leading uphill and away from the road. Turn left on to the B828, continue along this road then turn left on to a forest road with a waymark indicating hill access to Ben Donich.

Wade was appointed Commander-in-Chief for Scotland and between 1726 and 1737 he built more than 250 miles (402km) of roads through the Highlands. Construction, all of it by soldiers, was hard, back-breaking work. First the turf and topsoil was removed, then the soldiers dug until they hit rock or stone. This was levelled using a sledgehammer or, if the stones were too large,

WHAT TO LOOK OUT FOR

Check along the line of the military road to see if you can spot the line of banks constructed from the removed topsoil and the remains of ditches dug by Major Caulfield's soldiers. You might also come across the odd section of road where the tarmac surface is worn through to the original surface below and get some idea of how rough these former 'state-of-the-art' roads were.

REST AND BE THANKFUL

they were blasted with powder. To complete the job, 18in (45cm) of gravel was laid on top of the foundation, then topsoil used to build retaining banks. Finally ditches were dug to ensure good drainage and to keep the surface free from flooding. On a good day an average soldier could construct 4ft 6in (1.37m) of road.

Turn left at the next waymarker and continue on another forest road. Go through a gate and walk until you reach a fork in the road. Go left, along forestry roads with a superb view of the old military road below you to the left.

Wade's roads were a huge success, but not initially as he had imagined. During the 1745 Jacobite rising, Bonnie Prince Charlie used them to move his own forces south at a rapid pace, defeating all before him. He got as far as Derby and it is conceivable that had he continued to London the House of Hanover would have fallen. However, taking bad advice, he retreated instead of advancing and was eventually defeated at Culloden in 1746.

The forest road heads steadily downhill then turns left on to a bridge over the Croe Water. At the T-junction just after the bridge, turn left again on to the Old Military Road. This section was once the main road here until the A83 was built higher up the hillside, so the surface is relatively modern, unlike other sections of military road found elsewhere in Scotland. Go through a gate, then cross a stile at another and continue along the road, which is fairly flat at this point, but in the distance you will see it climb up, back to the car park.

After Culloden, Wade's former assistant Major William Caulfield continued the programme of road building. He began his work in Argyll in 1746 and, up until his death in 1767, Caulfield built over 800 miles (1,287km) of roads, over three times the amount constructed by his former boss, yet it is Wade's name that is still linked to those early roads.

Caulfield continued to work on the Dumbarton to Inveraray road in 1747. The following year his men reached the summit of the Rest and Be Thankful. As you cross the last two stiles then follow the road as it turns and climbs steeply, you'll realise why it bears that name. At the top, cross a stile to re-enter the car park and see the stone erected in 1768 by the soldiers who repaired this section.

Overleaf: Looking down over the Rest and Be Thankful Pass (Walk 45).

From Puck's Glen to the Benmore Botanic Garden

The story of James Duncan, the man who altered the Cowal landscape.

WALK 46

DISTANCE *4 miles (6.4km)* MINIMUM TIME *2hrs 30min*

ASCENT/GRADIENT *459ft (140m)* ▲▲▲ LEVEL OF DIFFICULTY +++

PATHS *Mainly forest roads and well-made footpaths, 1 stile*

LANDSCAPE *Woodland*

SUGGESTED MAP *OS Explorer 363 Cowal East*

START/FINISH *Grid reference: NS 142855*

DOG FRIENDLINESS *Keep dogs on lead*

PARKING *Car park at Benmore Botanic Garden*

PUBLIC TOILETS *At Benmore Botanic Garden*

Better known as the Younger Botanic Garden, after Harry George Younger who gifted his estate to the nation in 1925, the Benmore Botanic Garden is 120 acres (48.5ha) of the former estate. Extensive development, since it became part of the Royal Botanic Garden, Edinburgh, has made it world famous for its plant collections. The remainder of the estate, including Puck's Glen, belongs to the Forestry Commission and their afforested hillsides provide a splendid backdrop to the garden's formal collections. Yet none of this would exist without the passionate commitment of a self-made Victorian merchant, James Duncan.

Transforming the Landscape

Duncan, who made his fortune from sugar refining at Greenock, purchased the Benmore Estate in 1870 and laid the foundations of the gardens. When Duncan came to Benmore the landscape was bare and uninteresting. He immediately extended the former Tower House to create the main part of Benmore House. Around the formal gardens he constructed countless ranges of heated glasshouses and, overhanging a ravine in Glen Massan, he established a fernery, the remains of which are still visible today. Acting on the advice of Sir Joseph Hooker, Director of the Royal Botanic Gardens at Kew, Duncan began to plant the collections of shrubs and trees which would provide the basis of the gardens.

Cowal's Golden Gates

Extensive drainage systems were developed throughout the estate and trees were planted on the bare hillsides. Between 1871 and 1883 Duncan planted some 1,600 acres (648ha). The total area stretched from the Strone of Clyde to the head of Loch Eck. When he had done there were a total of 6,480,000 trees, which remain a major feature of the present landscape of this part of the Cowal peninsula. Duncan also commissioned the Golden Gates for the Paris Exhibition of 1865. Made from wrought iron and painted gold with his initials worked into them, they were eventually erected near Glen Massan in 1873. A sociable man, Duncan entertained frequently and welcomed many visitors to Benmore, including Sir Henry Morton Stanley, the explorer, and Charles Haddon Spurgeon, the Billy Graham of his day, who preached to a crowd of 7,000 in the grounds of Benmore in 1877.

Lasting Memorial

Duncan died at Spean Bridge, near Fort William on 12 August, 1905, aged 81. His body was brought back to Cowal and is buried in the historic churchyard at Kilmun. It lies under a pink granite slab on a high part of the steep graveyard with a view looking across the Holy Loch. At the southern limit of his Kilmun estate, on the Strone peninsula at Graham's Point, an obelisk was erected to Duncan's memory and on it can be found the only known likeness of the man, carved in stone. But his real memorial is the garden at Benmore and the surrounding landscape.

WALK 46 DIRECTIONS

❶ From the car park cross the A815 and follow the footpath past a waymarker for Black Gates. Pass a sign for the Big Tree Walk and turn right on to a surfaced lane. Continue along this lane for about 1 mile (1.6km) and just after the parapet of a bridge is the first footpath, which leads to Puck's Glen on the left.

❷ There's a milestone here pointing to 'Dunoon Pier 6 miles'. Ignore this entrance and continue along the lane until you reach the car park. Turn left and along a footpath past the waymarker pole for Puck's Glen. Climb uphill on a steep path.

❸ At the top of the hill the path levels out then starts to head back downhill, rather steeply on a series of steps with handrails to the bottom of the gorge. A signpost found at a junction at the bottom of the steps points left for the lower gorge and right for the upper.

❹ Turn right, head downhill on another set of steps, then cross a bridge on the left and turn right to head along a footpath on the opposite side of the stream. Head

uphill, cross another bridge, then go past a series of small waterfalls. Eventually reach yet another bridge to cross before coming to a set of steps that takes you up a steep part of the hillside to another bridge at the top. After crossing it, the path levels out a bit and continues through the trees to then reach a T-junction with a forestry road.

❺ At the junction is a waymarker post. Turning right will lead you along a forest road to Kilmun Arboretum. However, for this walk you must turn left, following the signs for Black Gates. The Forestry Commission has installed a series of new footpaths and this route can be shortened by taking any of the downhill paths that you'll find to the left.

❻ Follow the signs to the left and go on to the path for Black Gates car park and, from there, return to the botanic gardens. Otherwise continue on the forest road until you reach a gate located near its end. Continue to reach a T-junction and then turn left on to the A815. Walk along here for 0.5 mile (800m) to return to the start and the car park at Benmore Botanic Garden.

Along the Crinan Canal and Around Mhoine Mhor

A lengthy but easy stroll along a 19th-century canal and around Scotland's last wild peat bog.

WALK 47

DISTANCE 8.25 miles (13.3km)   **MINIMUM TIME** 5hrs

ASCENT/GRADIENT 176ft (54m) ▲▲▲   **LEVEL OF DIFFICULTY** ✦✦✦

PATHS Canal tow path, country roads and farm tracks

LANDSCAPE Bog, hillside and pasture

SUGGESTED MAP OS Explorer 358 Lochgilphead & Knapdale North

START/FINISH Grid reference: NR 824908

DOG FRIENDLINESS Keep on lead near livestock

PARKING Dunardry Forest car park

PUBLIC TOILETS None en route

Built just over 200 years ago, the Crinan Canal, just 9 miles (14.5km) in length, with 15 locks, allows easy passage from Loch Fyne to the Sound of Jura, avoiding the lengthy voyage around the Mull of Kintyre. It was designed by John Rennie but later improved by Thomas Telford in 1817. Because it is 69ft (21m) above sea level it needs a constant supply of water to replenish it and its main channels are fed from seven reservoirs in the hills above. But as every single locking operation uses 66,000 gallons (300,000 litres) of water, there have been periods, particularly during long dry summers, when it has run out of water and been forced to close.

The Great Moss

Crinan Canal runs along the southern fringe of Moine Mhor, the Great Moss, one of the last wild, raised bogs in Britain and one of the oldest living sphagnum bogs in Europe. As plants die, their remains become peat. Older than Stonehenge but growing at a rate of only 0.03in (1mm) each year, Moine Mhor is 13ft (4m) deep and is part of a National Nature Reserve.

Abundant Birdlife

The moss can be visited at any time. A wooden walkway leads from the North Moss car park area and this is the best way to view it. It's a birders' paradise echoing with the distinctive cry of the curlew as it returns to breed each spring. Stonechats, resident year round, are joined by whinchats in summer and you may spot the odd osprey hunting fish in the River Add. Watch too for the hen harrier quartering the moss in search of a quick meal. During the seasons the bog changes colour as heathers and grasses bloom then fade away. Cranberries bear purple flowers in the spring and deep red berries in autumn. Carnivorous plants like the sundew lie in wait to catch unsuspecting insects in their sticky hairs.

Invaders from Ireland

In AD 500 the Scotti tribe from Antrim landed here. To the Scotti, the vast rock of Dunadd in the middle of this great bog would have been the obvious place on which to build their first fortress and settlement. So the rock became the early capital of Dalriada. Near the summit are rock carvings including the figure of a boar, which may have been the tribe's emblem and some faint lines of ogam (alphabet of straight lines) inscription. A basin and footprint carved from the rock were probably part of early coronation ceremonies. The first recorded coronation here was of Aedann mac Gabhran by St Columba in AD 574. Dunadd, capital of Dalriada until 900, is still regarded as one of the most important historic sites in Scotland.

WALK 47 DIRECTIONS

1 From the car park go down some steps, cross the road and turn left. Keep going until you reach a white cottage on your right. Turn right and on to a dirt track that runs behind the cottage, then go through a gap between the fence and a wall. Cross the canal

over Dunardry Lock and then turn left following the tow path.

2 Head along the tow path as far as Bellanoch Bridge and then turn right on to the road, cross over Islandadd Bridge and on to the B8025. This narrow, but not busy, road is long and straight and runs right through the Moine Mhor.

Keep going ahead for nearly 2 miles (3.2km) then turn right on to an unclassified road, which is signposted for Drimvore.

> ### WHILE YOU'RE THERE
> Moored at Inveraray is the *Arctic Penguin*, a three-masted schooner built in 1911. Step aboard and learn of the horrors on slave ships, the hardships faced by immigrants during the Highland Clearances and find out about the life of Inveraray writer, Neil Munro, the man who created the stories of the Clyde puffer the *Vital Spark* and her rascally skipper, Para Handy.

3 Follow this for about 1.75 miles (2.8km) as it runs through the National Nature Reserve and passes the farms of Dalvore and Drimvore. Finally reach a T-junction with the A816 and turn right. After 0.5 mile (800m) an Historic Scotland fingerpost will point you in the direction of Dunadd Fort.

4 Turn right here on to a long straight farm road and keep on it, passing the farm of Dunadd, until you reach the Historic Scotland car park. Make your way towards the hill on a well-trodden path, go past the house on the left and through a kissing gate. Continue on the path, following

> ### WHERE TO EAT AND DRINK
> Originally an 18th-century coaching inn, the Cairnbaan Hotel was adapted to cater to traffic on the new canal. After years of neglect it has been totally refurbished and today attracts visitors like former US President Bill Clinton. Food served covers everything from bar snacks to gourmet meals in the restaurant which uses mainly fresh, local produce and seafood.

the direction arrows, to emerge through a gap in some rocks within the outer ramparts.

5 Continue from here to the summit and after you have admired the views, seen the carvings and tried your own foot in the carved footprint, return by the same route to the car park. Leave it and turn right on to a farm track. Go through a gate then, almost immediately, go left through another gate and follow it as it curves left.

> ### WHAT TO LOOK OUT FOR
> Look for the remains of a boathouse beside locks 9 and 10. This is where *The Linnet* was kept during the winter months. She was a little steamer used to ferry holiday visitors along the canal. At Bellanoch look to see how the engineers cut the canal into the hillside when it proved impossible to lay a foundation on the Moine Mhor.

6 Another gate is encountered just before the road turns right and heads uphill. Continue following the road going through another gate until you reach the steading of Dunamuck farm. Turn left through the steading, go through a gate and then head downhill on a farm road, continuing along it until you reach a T-junction with the A816.

7 Turn right on to the road and follow it for about 0.5 mile (800m), then turn right on to the road signposted for Cairnbaan and Crinan. After 0.25 mile (400m) turn right towards Crinan. As the road turns left across the swing bridge keep walking straight ahead and on to the canal tow path. Follow this back to Dunardry Lock and retrace your steps to the car park.

The Neolithic Monuments of Kilmartin Glen

A short walk back in time to the stone shrines and monuments in the valley of the ghosts.

DISTANCE 3.5 miles (5.7km)   **MINIMUM TIME** 3hrs

ASCENT/GRADIENT Negligible ▲▲▲   **LEVEL OF DIFFICULTY** ✦✦✦

PATHS Boggy fields, old coach road and country lanes, 3 stiles

LANDSCAPE Pasture, hills, woodland

SUGGESTED MAP OS Explorer 358 Lochgilphead & Knapdale North

START/FINISH Grid reference: NR 835988

DOG FRIENDLINESS Dogs fine on route

PARKING Car park outside Kilmartin church

PUBLIC TOILETS Kilmartin House

Kilmartin Glen with its lush alluvial plains, easy landfalls on the coast near Crinan and an abundant supply of water has attracted human settlers since the earliest times. In around 5000 BC, nomadic hunter gatherers frequented this area but left little evidence of their presence other than piles of bones and shells in caves.

Early Settlers

The arrival of small groups of neolithic people from around 3000 BC provided the first lasting signs of habitation. These early settlers, farmers and skilled weavers and potters, cleared the ground for grazing and erected the first stone shrines and circles. What they were for is not certain, but they were probably an early form of astronomical calendar for determining when to plant and harvest crops or to move cattle. They were probably also part of religious rituals closely related to the seasons and survival. Around Kilmartin Glen, 25 different sites of standing stones have been found. Some are simple arrangements, others single stones, while in Temple Wood the monument consists of two stone circles.

Great Monuments

Later, Bronze Age people were responsible for the monuments that can still be seen in the prehistoric linear cemetery, built over the course of 1,000 years, that runs for a mile (1.6km) down the glen. Each of the huge stone-lined burial chambers is slightly different in design and construction.

The Glebe Cairn, which looks like a pile of boulders with a cap stone, is situated near the church and is typical of the burial cairns of the period 1700–1500 BC. At the centre of this cairn were two stone cists for the burials and these contained pottery and a necklace of jet beads. The next tomb south from here, known as the North Tomb, has been rebuilt over a modern shelter that allows access through a hatch and contains a large slab carved with pictures of axe heads and cupmarks. The last cairn in this direction, the South Cairn is the earliest and was originally a chambered tomb dating from 4000 BC.

KILMARTIN GLEN

In the Iron Age, warring tribes ringed the glen with hill-forts and it was on one of these, at Dunadd, that the Scotti tribe from Ireland founded their capital in the 6th century AD (see Walk 47). St Columba came to Kilmartin in the 6th century AD and established the first Christian church here.

Within Kilmartin parish church can be found relics from a later age. The ornately carved Kilmartin Cross depicts one of the most moving images of Christ to have survived from the early Scottish Christian Church and the churchyard has one of the finest collections of ornately carved medieval gravestones in Scotland.

WALK 48 DIRECTIONS

❶ From the car park, visit Kilmartin church to marvel at the stones and see the Kilmartin Cross. Leave the church, turn left and walk along the road past Kilmartin House, exit the village and head downhill towards a garage on the left. Just before the garage turn left, go through a kissing gate and head across the field to the Glebe Cairn.

❷ From the cairn head half right, across the field to cross a stile. In wet weather this can be very boggy so stout footwear is advisable. Cross the stream by a bridge. Go through a gate and turn left on to the old coach road. Follow this to the next cairn. Go left over a stile and follow the path to visit the cairn.

❸ Return to the road and turn left, continuing to the next cairn. After exploring this, follow the coach road to Kilmartin school, where the route becomes a metalled road. Go through a crossroads, past Nether Largie farm and, ignoring the cairn on the left, continue a short distance to Temple Wood ahead on the right.

❹ Go through a gate on the right into Temple Wood, then return by the same route. Turn right on to the road and continue until you reach a T-junction. Turn left and

walk along this road until you come to a sign on the right for Ri Cruin Cairn. Cross the wall via a stile and proceed along the well-defined path to see the ancient monument.

❺ Return by the same route and turn right on to the road. Follow it to a T-junction then turn left and keep straight ahead until you reach the car park at Lady Glassary Wood. Opposite this, take a path to the left signposted to Temple Wood. Cross a bridge, go through a gate and head towards the standing stones.

❻ Turn right and walk across the field away from the stones towards a wood. Go through a gate and follow the fenced path to Nether Largie Cairn. From here continue along the fenced path, go through another gate and turn right on to the road. Continue past Nether Largie farm and Kilmartin school and then retrace your steps back to reach Kilmartin church and the car park at the start.

On to New Poltalloch

A walk to the faded ruin of a Victorian state-of-the-art dream.
See map and information panel for Walk 48

DISTANCE 6.25 miles (10.1km)	**MINIMUM TIME** 4hrs 30min	
ASCENT/GRADIENT Negligible ▲▲▲	**LEVEL OF DIFFICULTY** ✦✦✦	

WALK 49 DIRECTIONS
(Walk 48 option)

On reaching the T-junction at Point **A**, go straight ahead, past the lodge cottage on your right and proceed along a dilapidated estate road. Turn right at a T-junction and walk along this road, through stone gateposts next to a church.

The Church of St Columba was built in 1854 by the noted English church architect Thomas Cundy, Junior. It's his only work in Scotland and had stained-glass windows by William Wailes.

Return to the road and contine along it to reach a gate in the fence. Go through this, turn right, then head across an open field towards New Poltalloch house.

This enormous pile was built in 1849, in the neo-Jacobean style, by the famous Scottish architect William Burn, the most sought-after architect of his time and a pioneer of the Scots Baronial style. It cost Neil Malcolm, the owner, £100,000 – a colossal sum at the time – yet it stood for just over 100 years. Originally it was called Calltuinn Mór, the place of the great hazel trees, to distinguish it from the previous Poltalloch but soon became known simply as New Poltalloch.

There is a gate to the left of the house that gives access to what was once the garden but as this is very overgrown it is recommended that you do not enter. Under no circumstances whatsoever should you venture inside the old house. The floors have gone, the interior is unsafe and there is the possibility of falling masonry – all making it best admired from a distance.

When you have finished looking at it, retrace your steps across the field, go back through the gate and turn right on to the estate road.

Look back along the track for a splendid view of the ruin, its walls intact but with grasses, plants and trees growing from them and from the interior. By the 1950s the house was no longer, in 1957 the roof was removed to avoid high taxes and in no time the building was effectively dead. Nowadays, the local farmer stores large plastic-wrapped bales of hay in front of it rather spoiling the view in winter. By summer they will mostly have gone.

Follow the road through the estate until it reaches a T-junction beside East Lodge. Turn left on to the main road and walk along it to the next junction (Point **B**) where you will rejoin the main walk.

Overleaf: The Templewood Stone Circle in Kilmartin (Walks 48 and 49)

Carradale Forest Walk

A gentle stroll above the home of Naomi Mitchison.

DISTANCE 6 miles (9.7km)	**MINIMUM TIME** 3hrs

ASCENT/GRADIENT 410ft (125m) ▲▲▲ **LEVEL OF DIFFICULTY** +++

PATHS Forest roads, some forest paths and shingle beach, 1 stile

LANDSCAPE Forest, hillside, beach, pasture

SUGGESTED MAP OS Explorer 356 Kintyre South

START/FINISH Grid reference: NR 801381

DOG FRIENDLINESS Good walk for dogs

PARKING Network Carradale Visitor Centre

PUBLIC TOILETS At visitor centre

WALK 50 DIRECTIONS

Carradale, on the Mull of Kintyre, is where novelist Naomi Mitchison (1897–1999) and her husband Dick came to live in 1937. They bought Carradale House and Naomi spent most of her life here. A prolific writer, she continued to work well into her 80s and died at Carradale when she was 101.

From the visitor centre go past the interpretation boards, up wooden steps and turn left at the green waymarker pole. Go uphill through a wood, then turn left where the path meets a forest road. Follow the blue and red waymarker poles.

Mitchison was born in Edinburgh in 1897, educated at the Dragon School, Oxford and following in the footsteps of her famous father, the physiologist, J B S Haldane, went on to the university to read science. She abandoned her studies to enter nursing and in 1916 married Dick Mitchison, a barrister who later became a Labour politician.

Pass the waymarked turning for the red walk and continue along the forest road for about a mile (1.6km). Look out for some unusual shrubs including quince bushes and a profusion of wild flowers, particularly red campion, growing by the side of the road. Eventually reach a gate across the road. Cross here by a stile to arrive at a car park which is an alternative start to the walk.

When the Mitchisons lived in London, their house at Hammersmith was famous for its hospitality. The list of their visitors and friends reads like the literary *Who's Who* of the day and included Adlous Huxley, E M Forster,

WHILE YOU'RE THERE

Don't miss the fascinating displays at the Network Carradale Visitor Centre which chart the history of the area from prehistoric times to the present day. The sea and fishing are both covered in depth and it's the best place to come to learn about the local wildlife and forestry.

CARRADALE FOREST

sea to Arran. At the top, a little to the left of the footpath, is a strategically placed picnic table.

A P Herbert and Wyndham Lewis. When they moved to Carradale, the parties continued and it was not unusual for Naomi to be found typing away on an old battered typewriter surrounded by an army of visitors and children.

WHAT TO LOOK OUT FOR

Look across the water to Arran. From the forest road above the beach and the beach itself you will have a clear view of where the Highland Boundary Fault divides the island with the hilly, Highland area to your left and the flatter Lowlands to the right.

Turn right at the car park in the direction indicated by a fingerpost for the Kirnashie Walk. Continue along an old farm track uphill following blue waymarkers. When the track rejoins the forest road, keep right.

Naomi wrote more than 90 books on subjects ranging from Arthurian legend to science fiction. In her most controversial work, *We Have Been Wanted*, this noted feminist explored the whole gamut of sexual behaviour. Rejected by several publishers and subjected to censorship it was finally published in 1935.

When the road forks, go right and continue on this forest road until you encounter a blue waymarker on the right. Turn on to a footpath that heads uphill to reach the highest point of the walk with magnificent views over the

Actively involved in the local community, Naomi represented the area on the local council and was responsible for instigating the improvements to the harbour. Although Carradale House was regarded as an intellectual centre for young left-wing men and women, Naomi had a wide circle of friends drawn from all sections of society, and there was every possibility that they would find themselves in the company of ghillies, fishermen and locals from the surrounding village.

From the picnic table a well-made, new footpath heads downhill and to the south. On a clear day there are excellent views of the Firth of Clyde and Ailsa Craig, source of the world's curling stones. Pass a junction with a fingerpost indicating the way to Deer Hill.

Naomi was awarded a life peerage for her services to literature in 1964 but probably valued her appointment as 'mother' and advisor to the Baktgatla tribe of Botswana more.

WHERE TO EAT AND DRINK

The tea room at the visitor centre serves satisfying home-made soups, sandwiches and a host of hot main meals and, snacks. It also doubles as a gift shop for local souvenirs.

When the footpath stops at a T-junction with a lane, turn right then at the next junction keep right again. Follow this road uphill into the trees until you reach the sign for the Network Centre.

Turn left here and return to the visitor centre.

Walking in Safety

All these walks are suitable for any reasonably fit person, but less experienced walkers should try the easier walks first. Route finding is usually straightforward, but you will find that an Ordnance Survey map is a useful addition to the route maps and descriptions.

RISKS

Although each walk here has been researched with a view to minimising the risks to the walkers who follow its route, no walk in the countryside can be considered to be completely free from risk. Walking in the outdoors will always require a degree of common sense and judgement to ensure that it is as safe as possible.

- Be particularly careful on cliff paths and in upland terrain, where the consequences of a slip can be very serious.

- Remember to check tidal conditions before first walking on the seashore.

- Some sections of route are by, or cross, busy roads. Take care and remember traffic is a danger even on minor country lanes.

- Be careful around farmyard machinery and livestock, especially if you have children with you.

- Be aware of the consequences of changes in the weather and check the forecast before you set out. Carry spare clothing and a torch if you are walking in the winter months. Remember the weather can change very quickly at any time of the year, and in moorland and heathland areas, mist and fog can make route finding much harder. Don't set out in these conditions unless you are confident of your navigation skills in poor visibility. In summer remember to take account of the heat and sun; wear a hat and carry spare water.

- On walks away from centres of population you should carry a whistle and survival bag. If you do have an accident requiring the emergency services, make a note of your position as accurately as possible and dial 999.

COUNTRYSIDE CODE

- Be safe, plan ahead and follow any signs.

- Leave gates and property as you find them.

- Protect plants and animals and take your litter home.

- Keep dogs under close control.

- Consider other people.

For more information visit www.countrysideaccess.gov.uk/things_to_know/countryside_code and www.outdooraccess-scotland.com